Modern Witchcraft and Smudging

Unlock the Secrets of Divination, Spirit Guides, and Psychic Protection

© Copyright 2024 - All rights reserved.

The contents of this book may not be reproduced, duplicated, or transmitted without direct written permission from the author.

Under no circumstances will any legal responsibility or blame be held against the publisher for any reparation, damages, or monetary loss due to the information herein, either directly or indirectly.

Legal Notice:

This book is copyright protected. This is only for personal use. You cannot amend, distribute, sell, use, quote, or paraphrase any part or the content within this book without the consent of the author.

Disclaimer Notice:

Please note the information contained within this document is for educational and entertainment purposes only. Every attempt has been made to provide accurate, up-to-date, and reliable complete information. No warranties of any kind are expressed or implied. Readers acknowledge that the author is not engaging in the rendering of legal, financial, medical, or professional advice. The content of this book has been derived from various sources. Please consult a licensed professional before attempting any techniques outlined in this book.

By reading this document, the reader agrees that under no circumstances is the author responsible for any losses, direct or indirect, which are incurred as a result of the use of the information contained within this document, including, but not limited to, errors, omissions, or inaccuracies.

Your Free Gift
(only available for a limited time)

Thanks for getting this book! If you want to learn more about various spirituality topics, then join Mari Silva's community and get a free guided meditation MP3 for awakening your third eye. This guided meditation mp3 is designed to open and strengthen ones third eye so you can experience a higher state of consciousness. Simply visit the link below the image to get started.

https://spiritualityspot.com/meditation

Or, Scan the QR code!

Table of Contents

PART 1: MODERN WITCHCRAFT 1
    INTRODUCTION 2
    CHAPTER 1: WITCHCRAFT THROUGH THE AGES 3
    CHAPTER 2: WITCHCRAFT FESTIVALS AND BELIEFS 12
    CHAPTER 3: THE ELEMENTS 22
    CHAPTER 4: GODS AND GODDESSES IN WITCHCRAFT 32
    CHAPTER 5: TAROT CARDS 47
    CHAPTER 6: RUNIC DIVINATION 55
    CHAPTER 7: CRYSTAL DIVINATION 68
    CHAPTER 8: LUNAR MAGIC 79
    CHAPTER 9: SPIRIT GUIDES 89
    CHAPTER 10: RITUAL MAGIC 99
    BONUS CHAPTER: THE HERBAL GLOSSARY 106
    CONCLUSION 109
PART 2: SMUDGING 110
    INTRODUCTION 111
    CHAPTER 1: THE POWER OF SMUDGING 113
    CHAPTER 2: IDENTIFYING NEGATIVE ENERGY 123
    CHAPTER 3: BEFORE YOU START 133
    CHAPTER 4: HERBS, RESINS, AND OILS 142
    CHAPTER 5: HOW TO SMUDGE 155
    CHAPTER 6: SMUDGING ALTERNATIVES 166
    CHAPTER 7: CRAFTING YOUR SUPPLIES 176

CHAPTER 8: PSYCHIC PROTECTION METHODS 184
CHAPTER 9: CRYSTALS AND SMUDGING 195
CHAPTER 10: HEALING WITH SMUDGING 207
CONCLUSION 216
HERE'S ANOTHER BOOK BY MARI SILVA THAT YOU MIGHT LIKE 219
YOUR FREE GIFT (ONLY AVAILABLE FOR A LIMITED TIME) 220
REFERENCES 221
IMAGE SOURCES 231

Part 1: Modern Witchcraft

Unlocking the Secrets of the Norse Runes, Divination, Spirit Guides, Tarot Reading, Moon Spells, and Magic Rituals

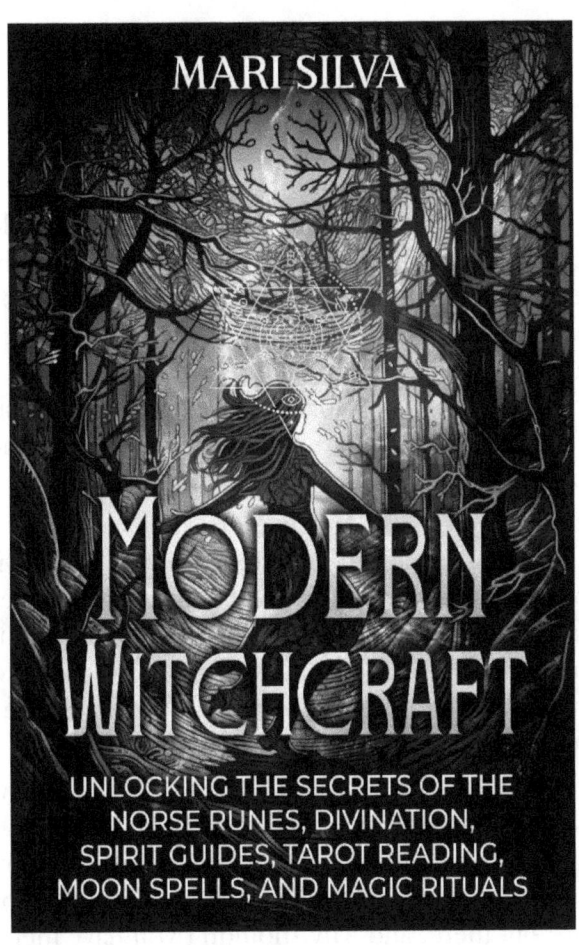

Introduction

Don't we all deserve a bit of magic in our lives? Have people become so focused on science and technology that they have lost the ability to think beyond the regular world and wonder what is out there in other realms? Human ancestors knew the importance of having an open mind and acknowledging that higher energies and beings exist outside their regular sphere of knowledge. They developed tools, spells, and rituals that asked these higher beings to come into their lives and bring their powerful energy with them.

Of course, some of these practices focused on negative energies. They were classed as Satanism or working with the devil, but these examples shouldn't give witchcraft a bad reputation. Modern society is beginning to seek out more supernatural forces and make them part of regular life, and why shouldn't you? Consider the word supernatural. Nature is amazing, and we all recognize that fact, so imagine tapping into a SUPER natural source. How amazing would that be?

You are about to discover how to be more in touch with yourself, your subconscious, and the array of natural and supernatural energy sources available. You have the control and means to explore these sources safely and with the knowledge that you can improve your life. Great things are out there, and why shouldn't you have them? Be part of the world of magic and discover your spirit team, who has been waiting for you since before your conception. They are benevolent and loving and will soon become part of your life. Are you ready to jump in and get started? Let's go!

Chapter 1: Witchcraft through the Ages

Witchcraft Timeline

Early mankind needed to find ways to survive. They needed shelter and food to keep their communities safe and healthy. Imagine being a hunter-gatherer back then, and you had to find ways to bring home food for your group. No information was available about how to trap your prey; you had to use the materials at hand. Early mankind used magic rituals involving the fertility of humans. They would attract animals by wearing the skins of their kills topped with antlers or horns to show their strength and leadership.

Magic men or shamans would hold elaborate ceremonies to thank the goddess of the hunt and the

Shamans held elaborate ceremonies to thank the goddess of the hunt.[1]

mistress of the herds and fish. One of the first depictions of early witchcraft was found in the French Pyrenees and named the Dancing Sorcerer. A magical being with human feet, the large round eyes of an owl, the genitalia of a large feline, and the tail of a horse or wild dog, all topped with the impressive antlers of a stag. The figure also had the front paws of a lion and was covered in animal skins. The image is believed to date back to 1400 BC and is believed to be the earliest record of witchcraft ever found.

As man became more developed and entered the Neolithic period, the Moon and the triple cycle of magic began to influence man's practices. Images of the triple goddess and the cycle of fertility became more important. Men had begun to rely more on agriculture to feed their communities, and the focus of their magic changed accordingly. A trio of stone statues dedicated to the Triple Goddess, the maiden, the mother, and the crone, were found in caves in France and are thought to have originated between 1100 BC and 1300 BC.

The more traditional timeline of witchcraft began back in Egypt and ancient Sumerians, where artifacts suggest that witchcraft and magic were important, and books of spells from around 3000 BC contained magic incantations and rituals dedicated to bringing back the dead and protecting the living.

The Bible also refers to multiple witches, divination, and the complex powers of magic. The Witch of Endor is called upon to consult with King Saul, and she predicts the death of Saul and his sons in a battle against the Philistines. The following day, Saul's sons were killed on the battlefield, and Saul was so distraught he took his own life. These references are believed to originate from around 900 BC. They are just a few of many references to the craft and magic that were common then.

Empress Wei, who ruled from 129 BC to 91 BC, was accused of practicing dark magic to help her get pregnant in China. She was exiled from the capital city along with hundreds of people helping her, and all of them were executed for their part in practicing witchcraft. The Romans and Greeks were also responsible for crediting witchcraft, and the Romans believed it was a certified practice that was a positive way to perform magic, while the Greeks viewed the craft more negatively.

In America, witchcraft was a heady mix of cultural beliefs, with Hoodoo, Voodoo, and Christianity all part of the melting pot. Slavery meant that African-based beliefs started to become part of the American culture and blended with more traditional beliefs to form the witchcraft that people believed in and performed. Many displaced cultural groups used witchcraft to make their lives more acceptable and fight back against their perceived place in society. The spells were often cast to improve their lives and fight against the endemic injustices the slaves faced and fought back against the masters and slave owners who controlled them. The Christian beliefs were upheld to mask the original craft and eventually became part of how magic is used today.

The Middle Ages was the most documented era of witchcraft, and many historians focused on the hunts and the trials that practitioners faced. In the 16th century and the years leading up to the era, magic was considered an acceptable practice and was part of regular worship and beliefs. Even the Church considered magic nothing more than superstition - nothing to be feared or even recognized - while the rest of the population believed and performed many forms of magic and witchcraft until the Church changed its perceptions.

In 1484, the Church changed its stance in an attempt to convince the populous that Pagan beliefs and magic were evil and that the only beings capable of such magic were God and the Holy Spirits. They issued an edict stating that witches were real and should be hunted down and held responsible for their evil practices. Throughout Europe, texts were written describing how to spot these evil witches and what to look for. Witch hunters were appointed to rid the communities of supposed witches and the people who supported them. Single older women were especially vulnerable to scrutiny, and women who lived alone were also under suspicion.

The rise of Protestantism also contributed to the furor, and both Catholics and Protestants formed committees and juries to try witches and send them to their fate. Religion played such a huge part in society that witches and their persecution were high on everyone's radar, leading to a system of fear and suspicion. A single rumor could start a major campaign against individuals or even families, and many people lived in fear of being persecuted. At the height of the witch panic, it is thought that between 40,000 and 50 000 people were executed, most female.

As the European panic subsided, the witch culture traveled across the ocean and found a new home in the Colonies. America was already a boiling pot of cultural influences when the town of Salem became the center of the new witchcraft superstitions. Three women were accused of being witches and started a maelstrom of accusations and persecution; these hearings are now called the Salem Witch Trials. The women were accused of casting spells that led to the possession of three girls in the town, which caused them to become the Devil's tools. The daughter of the Reverend Paris and her two cousins were acting irrationally and suffering from unexplainable fits, and the girls claimed that Sarah Good, a poor elder; Sarah Osbourne, a homeless beggar; and the Reverend's indentured servant Tituba were all guilty of witchcraft.

Tituba confessed to the crime and was pardoned, while Osbourne died before trial, and Good was hanged. She became the first "witch" to be executed on American soil, and her death led to a wave of paranoia and suspicion that spread through the Colonies rapidly. Over 200 people were accused, and at least 20 were executed. The situation was quelled in 1693 with a letter from Benjamin Franklin labeling the situation as ridiculous and having no basis in truth. In Europe, 1700 also marked an end to the superstitions and fear surrounding witchcraft. It led to laws being passed that stated that anyone who claimed to be a witch would be charged with fraud because witches weren't real and had no power.

While witchcraft never really disappeared, the hysteria surrounding it was dispelled, and other religions and beliefs became more prevalent. In the early 1920s, an English scholar who studied and taught Egyptology published a book called "The Witch Cult in Western Europe' in which she claimed that witches were practicing animal and child sacrifices and those covens led by the Devil himself were part of the culture and existed across Europe. However, she published a further book in the 1930s that changed her perceptions and proclaimed that witchcraft was the ancient religion that predated Christianity and should be included in modern culture.

It was in the 1950s that the resurgence of Paganism started to catch on with the emergence of Gerald Gardner and his book Modern Witchcraft. He started a movement known as Wicca and consulted with the infamous Aleister Crowley to create rituals, spells, and other magical pagan traditions that worked with the seasons, equinoxes, and solstices. In 1953 Gardner appointed an English woman, Doreen Valiente as his high priestess of the coven known as Bricketwood Coven. She was an influential figure who had been practicing magic since childhood and was an accomplished advocate of Wicca.

Doreen went on to become one of the most influential voices of modern magic, and she wrote five books about the craft. Her work encouraged readers to do more research and advocated that Wicca could be practiced by anyone and everyone without being initiated and part of the official Wicca movement. Her legacy was described as "The Mistress of Modern Magic," and she encouraged the growth of Wicca until her death in 1999.

Modern Witchcraft Today

Wicca and other pagan beliefs have become more popular since the 1970s, and more people are turning to alternative religions rather than conforming to traditional ones. They are embracing nature-based magic and using pagan traditions to mark the changes in seasons and how to live with the magic of nature. People are leaving more traditional religions and embracing spirituality instead. They prefer to distance themselves from established churches that have been connected to scandals and beliefs that limit what their followers can do. Religion is judgmental, and millennials aren't prepared to be told by anyone what they should do and what punishments they face if they choose another path.

Millennials are well-informed and unrestricted by their choices. They know what is out there and can connect to the rest of the world with just a click of a button. Information about Hinduism, Wicca, Buddhism, and other religions and belief systems is easily accessible, and they can chat with practitioners worldwide. This is both liberating and paralyzing, as too many choices could mean they fail to choose because they fear making the wrong choice. Spirituality, a blanket term, gives them the freedom to work with others dedicated to casting off consumerism and working together to make the world a better place.

Witchcraft has been expanded to include many different practices to suit modern society. New-age witches are everywhere, and they no longer have to fear society. They practice in full view or in their homes depending on their preferences and are part of the new belief system that is more inclusive and far thinking.

Types of Witches

First, let's eliminate the horror story image of witches with warty faces and scary green skin that are intent on capturing the innocent princess.

Witches aren't occult or servants of the Devil, but they are supernatural. What is supernatural? Traditionally supernatural means a phenomenon that is beyond the laws of nature and scientific understanding, but in witchcraft terms, it can be more literal. Witches are supernatural because they work with and understand the natural world's power and how to use them. Modern witches look like everybody else and are often accomplished healers who work with nature to bring magic to the world. They are not outcasts; they are accepted in society, and all identify with certain characteristics. Look at the list below and see if you can identify with witchcraft or if you recognize any that seem familiar.

Traditional Witches

Often referred to as folk witches, these practitioners will often work in covens and practice more traditional spells. They prefer to work with older spirits connected to their region and are knowledgeable about the craft through the ages. If you meet a traditional witch, you will learn a lot about the origins and history of witchcraft and the literature created.

Ceremonial Witches

These practitioners are more secretive than other witches who work with ceremonial magic. They believe in the power of high magic, and their practices have a certain pecking order. Ceremonial witches attain self-esteem from their magic and intend to become more accomplished and learned.

Kitchen Witches

One of the more popular forms of witchcraft involves performing magic in the heart of the house and the kitchen. Kitchen witches create potions and food to heal and bring luck and love to themselves and their loved ones. They will often be accomplished gardeners and have a sustainable source of ingredients in their homes. Kitchen witches work with seasonal ingredients and follow recipes passed down through their families for generations.

Green Witches

Also called forest witches, these practitioners work outside with the magic of nature. They have a deep knowledge of plants and herbs and a powerful connection with the elements. The green witch will often work with kitchen witches and collaborate to make healthy and magic dishes and potions from their ingredients.

Hearth Witches

Another form of the craft centers on the home. Everybody knows that the hearth is the traditional place in the home where the family gathers and shares their experiences. Hearth witches are often skilled crafters and use natural products and materials to create their magic. They use their skills to bring positive and healing energy to themselves and their homes. Even though most modern homes don't have traditional hearths, this kind of witchcraft is still effective and popular.

Hedge Witches

Although the name suggests some connection to greenery, the hedge means something different in magic. The hedge is the barrier between this world and the spiritual realm. Hedge witches have experienced communicators and will use their magic to speak to the spirits and bring their messages back to this world. They use astral traveling or lucid dreams to form their connections. They are adept at separating their soul from their physical body so it can travel between the two worlds.

Some cultures refer to this type of witch as a shaman, seidh, or an astral witch.

Cosmic Witches

These witches use astrology and astronomy to power their magic. They draw energy from the stars and the skies, using that energy to perform rituals and cast spells. Cosmic witches will study natal charts and use the alignment of the planets and stars to guide them during their work. Cosmic witchcraft involves a lot of details and appeals to people who believe in the power of the cosmos.

Augury Witches

These witches rely on their magic to see the future and divine what may occur in the future. They use omens, tarot cards, and other tools to seek signs, and they can also work with animals and the natural world. Augury witches often fall into trances and meditative states when they perform their magic and will work with the spirit world and nature to create their visions and messages,

Norse Witches

These witches follow the ancient Norse traditions and study Odin and Freya. The Norse religion of Asatru is filled with magical connections and powers that originated from the old Gods and Goddesses that form the beliefs they follow today. Asatru is popular because followers don't worship their deities. They believe they have human qualities and are as prone to making mistakes as regular men. Norse legends often depict them as drunken buffoons or brawling idiots who can be tricked and led astray. These human qualities make them some of the more approachable deities in pagan beliefs and help their popularity.

Elemental Witches

These witches work with elements and cast their spells using the power of nature. Later in the book, the elements and their place in witchcraft will be examined more closely.

Faery Witches

The Fae are mythical fairy-like creatures that appear in Celtic mythology and are representative of natural phenomena. The witches connect to the creatures and draw energy from them to fuel their magic. This type of practice is related to green witchery but concentrates on the faeries as well as the connection they have to nature.

Lunar Witches

Like cosmic witches, these practitioners focus on the skies, particularly the moon. They use rituals and spells filled with lunar energy, and the spells they cast will be explained later in the book.

Solar Witches

These witches use the sun's power to energize their tools and spells. They channel the sun to bring light and positivity to their magic. They will often perform their rituals or magic at sunrise or sunset so that these are enhanced by solar energy.

Sea Witches

These witches work with the power of water, especially the sea. They work with spirits and entities that live in the waves and have rituals that connect them to certain deities. Their environment often dictates the magic of sea witches, and they will also work using other bodies of water, such as lakes and rivers.

Secular Witches

These witches don't believe in divine blessings or powers. They have no connection to deities or religious bodies and believe solely in the power of ten natural worlds. This doesn't mean there aren't any secular religious witches. They may follow a religion but separate the two parts of their lives so magic and religion don't influence each other.

Chaos Witches

These witches embody the natural chaos of the world. They believe that creating loud and conflicting energies fuels their magic. Many witches practice in calm and serene conditions that help them connect to the spirits, but chaos witches do the opposite. They make loud noises and thrive on the energy that they create. They also work well with turbulent weather and love to perform rituals in storms and chaotic meteorological conditions. Beware the chaos witch, as they normally favor curses and hexes in their practice, so if you anger them, you may feel their wrath.

Eclectic Witches

These witches practice multiple kinds of magic and are always open to new ideas. Eclectic is an umbrella term to describe witches who embrace different forms of the craft. They understand that natural connections lead to commonalities in magic. For instance, the lunar witch and the sea witch will share certain energies because the lunar cycles affect the sea.

Whichever type of witch you identify with is fine. There are no hard and fast rules about your beliefs and where you draw your energy from. Maybe you practice a witchery style that isn't mentioned here. That's also okay; just like the regular world, labels are less important than intentions. Call yourself whatever you like, as witches are powerful and important no matter what.

Chapter 2: Witchcraft Festivals and Beliefs

What Is the Wheel of the Year?

The Wheel of the Year shows nature's cycles, which form the basis of magic.[2]

When people hear about pagan rituals and witchcraft, they often think of dark rituals in the winter and summer solstice celebrations offering worship to perform dark magic and to connect with otherworldly spirits. In reality, the real wheel of the year is much more than a pagan calendar. Its origins date to pagan and neopagan cultures, but its real meaning is much more concerned with divine creation and the cycles of nature, which form the basis of magic and witchcraft. If you genuinely want to understand how your ancestors celebrated the seasons and the changing conditions in which they lived, you need to study the wheel of the year and the celebrations it represents.

Why do you look at the calendar? Birthdays, holidays, dentist appointments, and other mundane reasons are the main reasons people keep calendars but imagine how it was in pre-Christian times before the technologically advanced era. People who lived millennia ago didn't have the benefit of electricity and other modern power to rely on. When it went dark, there were only candles and fire to illuminate their homes, and when the weather changed, they needed to know what would and wouldn't grow to feed themselves. They needed bountiful harvests, and their knowledge of the cyclical changes in nature had to be part of that process to produce the food they needed when the seasons were favorable.

The wheel of the year is divided into eight sabbats representing points of the year that mark a shift in the season. They each have individual powers and characteristics that are celebrated accordingly. Some are solstices, equinoxes, and cross-quarter days, which are important milestones throughout the calendar year. Imagine the excitement and joy the community would feel as winter ended and fresh buds and spring flowers emerged. Imagine the hope and wonder when their animals began to produce offspring that would put meat on the family table and ensure their survival for another year.

Today the wheel of the year is less important. People eat imported foods, and the only way the seasons affect their lives is through what clothing they wear. Modern pagans, Wiccans, and other witchcraft groups are different. They understand that the power of nature is still cyclical and that the rituals and magic of the wheel of the year can help people to learn more about the natural world and how to care for it. No matter how hard you try to understand it, humankind is intrinsically linked to nature, and it isn't healthy to disconnect from it. It is spiritually fulfilling to cast off modern ways and retune your mind to nature and its changing seasons, so the wheel of the year is an effective guide to honoring nature's cycles.

The Eight Sabbats

Let's start with perhaps the best-known sabbat, Samhain. This is where the wheel of the year begins and the cross-quarter day that people recognize that summer has gone and the nights are starting to draw in.

Samhain 31st October – 1st November

Samhain evolved into All Hallows Eve or Halloween in more modern times, and, in some countries, children go out in fancy dress to "trick or treat" their neighbors and receive sweets and treats from them. The more traditional way to celebrate Samhain was to slaughter animals and store them in preparation for winter and to preserve other foodstuffs. The feast of Samhain represented taking stock and preparing for the cold months.

Samhain is when the veil between the living and the spiritual world is at its thinnest, and beings from the other world can cross easily to enter the physical world. Bonfires would be lit to cleanse the area, and the celebrants would leave food and drink to feed the spirits who visited. The Catholic Church adopted Samhain as All Hallows' Eve to mark a day to celebrate the dead and remember their time on Earth.

It is a time for reflection and taking stock spiritually. At Samhain, celebrate the return of darkness and heightened spiritual connections. Use the celebrations to mark endings and new beginnings so you can start afresh.

Correspondences

Nature: Squash and zucchini, pine cones, fungi, mushrooms, root vegetables.

Symbols: Squash and pumpkins for carving, skeletons, trees, ancestors, and the crone.

Colors: Red, black, brown, orange, and yellow.

Use the ingredients to make hearty stews and meals for yourself and your family. Batch cook meals in the freezer and preserve vegetables from your garden or the kitchen, so you don't waste anything. Make jam from leftover fruit and store it in your cupboards for winter.

Samhain Ritual

Decorate a room with relevant correspondences and pictures of your relatives who have passed. Light a single red candle and close your eyes. Ask the spirits of your ancestors to visit you and share their guidance on your life. Ask them to give you advice about specific areas and send you messages. The veil between the two worlds is at its thinnest and makes it the perfect time to connect with them.

Winter Solstice 21st December

Also known as Yule, this is the darkest point of the wheel. In modern terms, the 21st of December is the shortest day of the year and marks the end of the shortening of the days and longer nights. The ancients knew how special this time of year was and celebrated accordingly. They gave gifts, forgave moral transgressions, and offered sacrifices and gifts to the God Saturn. This is a time for transformation and rebirth, so magic centers around these energies. While the rest of the world prepares for Christmas, you can celebrate Yule by burning a Yule log and inviting your friends and families to your home for lavish feasts.

The winter solstice is a time for rest, and pagans look to nature for inspiration. The bees have sealed their hives and trees are bare and perennial plants are taking their nourishment from stored nutrients. Nature is taking a break, and you should do the same. Take the time to nourish your soul and mind by snuggling under blankets and reading. Eat heart food and replenish your energy.

Correspondences

Nature: Citrus, cinnamon, peppermint, rosemary, and sage

Symbols: Pine tree, holly, stars, logs, the hearth, reindeer, and candles

Colors: Red, gold, green, white, and silver

Yule Ritual

Light a red and green candle and ask the spirits to help you find peace. Close your eyes and reflect on the last year and what you achieved. Imagine a white light surrounding you and keeping you free from harm. Now take two deep breaths and feel peace descend and fill your body. Extinguish the candles and thank the spirits for their presence.

Imbolc 31st Jan – 1st Feb

This is the sabbat that celebrates the start of spring for pagans. As snowdrops break through the hard soil and the first signs of new life appear, it is time to celebrate rebirth. The sun has started to appear for longer, and it is time for you to welcome new projects and plant the seeds of intent. In agriculture, it is time to prepare the ground for the new planting cycle, and the same principles apply to witchcraft. Take the time to cleanse your magic tools and recharge them in the sun or moonlight.

Imbolc is the time to welcome back the light and celebrate the goddess, Brigid. She is the symbol of new life and is represented by a small cross made from woven rushes and placed at the door to the home. Connect to her by creating an altar related to Imbolc and asking her to send energy and love to you. She is the goddess of creativity and healing, so honor her by writing a poem or planting seeds to represent the rebirth of nature.

This is a magical time of the year and the perfect time to connect to nature. Grow your own herb garden or plant some hardy vegetables to celebrate your connection. Plant snowdrops and daffodils in your garden, or visit areas of natural beauty to welcome back the light into your life.

Correspondences

Nature: Snowdrops, daffodils, crocus, new potatoes, spring vegetables, fish

Symbols: The cross, straw dolls, flowers

Colors: White, yellow, pale blue, orange, silver

Imbolc Ritual

Create a sacred space on your altar or table and set three candles upon it. One white, one orange, and one green work well, but you can use whichever candles you have on hand.

Light them and close your eyes as you ask the spirits for the gift of light.

"Light the fire within my heart and let the light guide me,
Step with me along the way and keep my spirit safe.
Shadows that have ruled the land will now be gone.

And from their darkness, spring has sprung
And with its life and energy,
Let my life be renewed and bring me strength and force."

When the candles have burned away, thank the spirits and finish the ritual.

Ostara or the Spring Equinox 21st March

Now nature is balanced, and there is an equal amount of light and darkness every day. Blossoms start to appear on the trees, and the chilly air of winter is but a memory. This is a time for hope, optimism, rebirth, and celebration. Ostara has inspired a lot of Easter traditions and customs, like egg hunts and the Easter bunny. Celebrate by creating colorful food and drinks that are filled with goodness. Share your home with friends and family and encourage crafting and nature hunts. Hide eggs in the garden so children and adults can have fun finding them and eating the spoils of their labor.

Correspondences

Nature: Daffodils, tulips, crocus, ducks, eggs, rabbits

Symbols: Eggs, hares, rabbits

Colors: Pastel yellow, pale blue, sea green, pink, purple

Ostara Ritual

Decorate your altar with eggs and rabbit toys, and place two yellow candles on the surface. Light them and ask the spirits to show you the power of rebirth. Ask them to fill your life with light and happiness and bring energy to you and your magic. Blow out the candles and thank the spirits for their assistance.

Beltane 1st May

This is truly the start of summer; the light expands, and long days beckon. Nature displays her nurturing side, and the world is green and abundant. The ancient pagans would have been filled with hope for the future, and two fires would be lit to bring cleansing smoke to their celebrations. Farmers would walk the cattle between the two fires before being led to summer pastures to graze. Cows would then jump over straw set on fire to prevent the fairies from stealing their milk.

Fires are a major part of Beltane celebrations, and young couples would leap over the flames to ensure conception. As the fires burned away, pregnant women would jump across them to protect their unborn children and bring them luck. The cooled embers would then spread across the sprouting crops to protect and encourage them to grow.

In modern times the celebration changed to May Day, but many old traditions still apply. The maypole can often be seen in village squares or smaller communities where the population gathers and dance. Maidens would dance and encourage young men to join them, while others would sell garlands of flowers to boost their dowry. May and Beltane are about nature coming to full bloom and is often associated with sexuality and conception.

Cast magic based on growth and fruition and celebrate the new life that is springing forward. Create a May doll dressed in white and decorated with flowers to adorn your house. Decorate your home with fresh flowers and bright ribbons to create a fun atmosphere, and invite your friends to BBQs and drinks so you can all look forward to summer together. Organize nature walks with friends and take notebooks and a pen to record and draw what you see.

Correspondences
Nature: Hawthorne, bluebells, berries, white roses, wisteria
Symbols: Garlands, flowers, the Maypole, the maiden, white flowers
Colors: Pale green, pastel yellow, pink, white, silver

Beltane Ritual
Decorate your altar with fresh flowers and white candles. Light the candles and ask for the spirits to bring love and romance to your life or to strengthen any current relationship. Ask for warmer and brighter weather to connect with nature.

Litha or the Summer Solstice 20th-21st June

The peak of the wheel. The days are at their longest, and the sun is strong. This is the sabbat to honor solar energy and perform magic connected with its power. The sun is the primary reason humans have life, so remember to honor the life-giving properties, and it is a time for outdoor celebrations with groups of people sharing their food. It is also a time for love and procreation, so celebrate your relationships and take advantage of the great outdoors.

Use natural ingredients to create tasty Litha treats like honey cakes or lavender cookies. Build a bonfire and celebrate the night sky in the warmth of its light. Litha is the time for exploration, so visit places that inspire you and bring you happiness. Go to the beach, feel the sun on your face as you dip your toes into the sea, and thank nature for its warmth. Go foraging for food and learn about the different bounties out there. Remember to check if plants are edible before you use them in your kitchen. Pick fruit from the elder tree and dry the fragrant white flowers to make cordial for fresh drinks or fry them in batter to make tasty fritters.

Correspondences

Nature: Elderflower, roses, lavender, tomatoes, spring onions, lettuce

Symbols: The sun, shells, fire, flowers, garlands,

Colors: Bright pink, yellow, gold, orange, turquoise, aquamarine

Litha Ritual

Take time to connect with nature by creating an altar in the garden. Add a bowl of fresh water, a yellow candle, and fresh flowers. Light the candle and close your eyes. Breathe in the fresh air and ask nature to bathe you in her light and positivity. Ask the spirits to bring prosperity and abundance to your life and inspire you to be more creative. Extinguish the candle and leave the altar with thanks and hope.

Lammas 1st August

The fruit is ripe, the crops are grown, and it is time to reap the rewards. Harvest is upon us, and it's time to enjoy nature's abundance. In magic terms, this means it's time to spend time with your loved ones and be powered by their energy. Your psychic abilities will be enhanced, and you will be more connected to high vibrations. Your connections will be at their best, and this is the time to connect with your spirit guides and ask them to guide you. Traditional English harvest festivals represent the way ancient pagans celebrated Lammas, where they brought gifts for the less fortunate members of the community.

Choose Lammas to volunteer your time at local homeless shelters or donate to charity. Clear out your home and prepare it for the long months ahead. Donate the items you clear out and be grateful for your bounty and the earth's sustenance.

Correspondences

Nature: Vegetables, apples, wheat, corn, mature roses

Symbols: An ear of corn, the scythe, and bread

Colors: Deep pink, gold, brown, amber, and red

Lammas Ritual

Lammas is the perfect time to try home baking, especially if you haven't done so before. Bake a simple loaf of bread and then place it on your altar. Break the bread into four quarters and place them at the points of the compass. Bless the bread and sprinkle it with water before sharing it with your family.

Mabon the Autumn Equinox 21st September

This is the final harvesting cycle when the last of the crops are brought in from the fields, and you begin to prepare for winter. The daylight hours are getting shorter, and the air is filled with a hint of frost. Mabon is the time to celebrate those last sunny days of summer and build fires to feast around. The leaves are falling, and it's time for you to shed some of your layers. Concentrate on self-doubt and how to get rid of it. Use magic to increase your self-confidence and love. Start a journal and make a wish list of things you will do in the following year.

Correspondences

Nature: Acorns, dried leaves, pine cones, horse chestnuts,

Symbols: Piles of harvested vegetables, leaves, the scythe, and bread

Colors: Red, orange, amber, brown, yellow, gold, and purple

Mabon Ritual

Cover your altar with a golden cloth and place two red candles on top. Use paper and pen to list the things you want to change about yourself. Light the candles and burn the paper safely as you ask the spirits to guide you. Watch the ashes fall to the floor and imagine your worst habits falling away from you. Extinguish the candle and thank the spirits for their attendance.

The wheel of the year may not be as important to our regular lives as it was for our ancestors, but it is a strong link to nature and the past. Perhaps it will alert you to the changing seasons and make you more in tune with how nature functions to bring food and sustenance to the table. Perhaps it will give you more reasons to connect with your friends and the spiritual world so you feel their energy and connection. It will remind you that cycles are part of life and that people need to flow with energy and be part of the wonder of nature.

Chapter 3: The Elements

There is a common belief that there are five fundamental elements in witchcraft and regular life, but this chapter includes an extra element that is often overlooked. The sixth element will bring increasing levels of power to your craft and will help you find different ways to use it in your work. In the popular game *World of Warcraft*, the power of the sixth element is apparent and forms part of weaponry - scientific studies use the element freely. What is this powerful element? Read on and discover exactly what you have been missing out on.

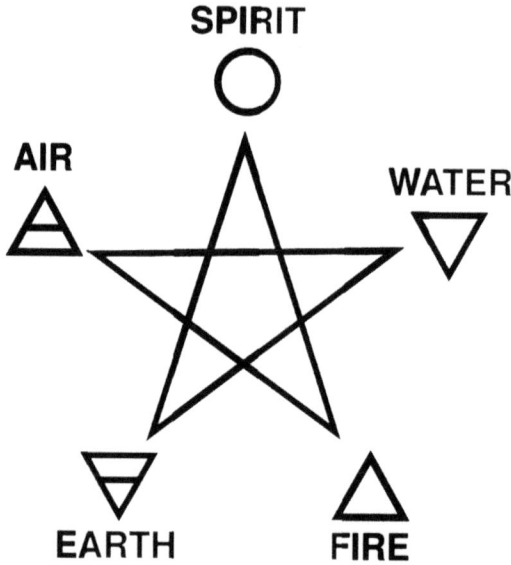

The 5 fundamental elements.'

The Six Elements and How to Invoke Them in Your Rituals

In witchcraft, many practitioners use the four cardinal points to bring power to their magic, and they call upon the four pillars to create a protective space and foundations to ensure their work is safe. The four pillars are Willingness, Knowing, Daring, and the Time of silence, but that's another branch of magic. The elements you are studying can be used alongside these strong foundations and pillars to create magical cohesive energy to fuel your spells and protect you as you work.

Many witches are familiar with the regular five elements. Still, the addition of the sixth will help you grow and become more effective, so let's explore the elements and how to bring them into your magical world.

Element: Air

Cardinal Direction: East

Corresponding Color: White or yellow

Pillar: Knowledge

The air brings energy through the slightest breeze or the most powerful gale. It moves seeds and pollen through the air to bring life to the earth. Air brings intelligence, speech, movement, and countless other strengths to your magic. Air is light and invisible, but it contains amazing strength and brings strength to spells for travel, knowledge, and finding what is lost. The element of air creates the image of cloudy skies. It represents mountain tops and windswept plains that inspire you to see the world.

Air spells are best performed in spring and include the use of wands and crystals like citrine. Use incense and smudge sticks to invoke the air element and appeal to the deities you follow to join you in your craft. Air deities include a modern figure from American folklore, Aradia, who appears in the popular 1899 work, The Gospel of Witches. Her name also connects to a powerful Italian goddess; she is a key figure to work with when using the element air in your spells.

Air Spells

The Creativity and Wind Magic Spell

This will help you release your inner creativity and increase your personal strength. It is an effective way to identify your strengths and weaknesses and allow for personal growth. This spell gives you an insight into your own form and lets you connect to the elements and feel their power.

What You Need:

- Freshly-cut spring flowers
- Wind instrument (anything will do, a penny whistle or a cheap recorder works just as well as expensive and ornate flutes)
- Freestanding yellow candle
- Sage smudge stick

Choose a place where you connect to nature and cleanse it with your sage. Seat yourself on the floor and place the candle in front of you. Light the candle and place your wind instrument between yourself and the candle.

Say the words,

"Yellow candle in the wind and air, bring creativity to share. Show me how to find my inner artist and bless my work with originality and love."

Visualize how this will manifest. Are you a painter or a writer? Do you want to do something physical like crafting or sculpting? If you are unsure, just close your eyes and let the element of air fill your lungs by breathing deeply and letting the air out slowly. Images should appear that help you identify what you are destined to achieve.

Pick up the instrument and play notes on it. Don't try and replicate a tune you already know. This is a spell for your creativity, not to celebrate someone else's work. Let the notes flow and float away on the wind as you hear the melody and bask in the sweetness and purity of the noise.

Imagine an instrument as a tool that draws in the energy of air and feel it fill your lungs with pure oxygen. Feel the energy fill you with hope and love and imagine your energy levels rising. Think back to the visualization and the creative activity you saw.

Set the instrument down, extinguish the candle, and thank the spirits and elements for their interactions before you leave. Go and begin the creative activity.

Smoke Air Travel Spell
What You Need:
- Feather
- A sprig of fresh mint
- Hand fan
- Small yellow bag

Crush the fresh mint by hand or using a pestle and mortar. Take a moment to breathe in the smell and let it fill your lungs and nose.

Take the feather in your hand and visualize where you want to travel to. Imagine the whole process, the packing, the journey, and eventually, arriving at your chosen destination. Throw the feather in the air and use the fan to keep it off the floor. Keep fanning until you feel the spell is finished, and catch the feather in your hand. Place the mint and the feather in the bag and carry it with you until you arrive at your chosen destination.

Element: Fire

Fire is a masculine element perfect for spells involving passion, sex, power, and strength.

Cardinal Point: South

Color: Red or orange

Solid Shape: Triangular

Pillar: Willfulness

Fire spells are mostly candle spells, but you can go bigger with burning rituals if you do them safely. Fire consumes and cleanses, and it is the source of food and water. It creates the fuel that fires humankind and gives light and heat to mankind. It brings drive and determination to your spells and ensures they will be more effective.

Fire spells are great for witchcraft newbies as they are impressive yet simple to perform. But it wasn't always so. Imagine your ancestors experiencing fire for the first time and the way it changed their lives. Now remember the phenomenon of wildfires and the terror they bring to the areas where they occur. Fire shouldn't be underestimated, and it should be respected and revered. When you use fire in your magic, it is simple to strike a match and produce instant flames but imagine how it feels to use flint and steel to create your elemental ingredient. Try and create fire with natural elements and feel the extra strength it brings to your magic.

Fire Banishment Spell

This spell is meant to get rid of the energies that are holding you back. Negativity from a past relationship or weaknesses you feel stop you from moving forward. Never use this spell to eliminate living objects or people; that is pushing the boundaries too far. If you have doubts about anything, this spell will clear them and give you the intuition to move forward and achieve your goals.

What You Need:

- Cauldron, this can be any size pot providing it is fireproof
- Paper and pencil
- BBQ starter gel
- Match or lighter

Take the paper and pencil and write a single word to represent what you want to banish. Is grief or sadness holding you back? Is doubt your anchor? Write the word clearly and with intent.

Fold the paper and place it in the cauldron. Add the flammable gel and light the match. Throw the match onto the gel and watch that initial burst of flame shoot up and light the room.

Say the words,

> *"Fire does burn the word so bright; it makes the issue leave my sight; no more will I have to fight; from this day forward, the world is right."*

Hold your hand over the cauldron when it is safe, and visualize what you want to banish. Imagine it as a solid form and see it disappear from the pot and float away from you. Now the spell is finished, and the energy has dispersed. Thank the spirits and the element for their help, and move on with your regular life.

Element: Water
Cardinal Direction: West
Color: Blue

Alchemic Symbol: Inverted triangle

Pillar: Daring

What do you think of when you hear the word water? Is it a cooling drink to quench your thirst or the hot water that cleanses you? Do you imagine the sea, amazing waves, and wildlife that populate the oceans? Maybe rivers and lakes or huge powerful waterfalls? Whatever you imagine, the power and strength of water is indisputable.

Water flows and changes to suit the vessel that holds it, and just one tiny drop can cause ripples that change the environment. Water is the grand force that creates canyons and gullies and is the element of our emotions. It represents the mysteries of life, and in magic, it is used to tap into the deepest secrets people hold beneath their cognizant selves. Use water to become more intuitive and allow yourself to become more malleable but retain your original form.

The beauty of the element water is its availability. Unlike fire, you don't have to create it, it is everywhere, and you choose which water is used. Start to connect to the element by appreciating it in all its forms. Raise your face to the skies as it rains and let cold snowdrops melt on you. Thank the elemental forces whenever you drink water or wash your hands.

The Water Protection Spell

What You Need:

- Water
- Sea salt
- Bowl. *(Don't use a kitchen bowl; use one that is solely for magic purposes to add intent and purity)*
- Fresh or dried mint or parsley

If you can, perform the spell near a body of natural water like a pond or lake. Create a circle of protection with your salt keeping some back for the spell. You can fortify the circle with eight stones to bring added protection.

Step into the circle and sit down with your supplies. Add the water, salt, and herbs, and start visualizing what you require from the spell. What do you want to protect? Your home, your family, yourself, or your partner? It can be anything that comes to mind. Imagine locking yourself in a small room with thick walls and solid doors that protect you. Now see yourself lying on the floor and surrounded by things that make you feel calm and at peace. This can be a litter of puppies or a warm blanket. The main thing is to feel protected. It doesn't matter about details; it's all about the sensation of feeling safe.

Now hold the bowl in front of you and gaze into the water. Let your fears flow into the water and be cleansed by salt and herbs.

Say the words,

"There is no cause for alarm; I am free from things that can harm; this water is my protection and will block evil before it has begun."

Now feel the negativity entering the bowl and becoming part of the water. You can further cleanse the solution with regular iodized salt and leave the liquid for a few moments. Remove the herb without touching the tainted water and bury it in the ground and say the words:

"Dear sprig of herb, I thank you, Keep me free from harm and safe and free."

The process can be repeated until you feel completely protected and safe from harm. When the spell is done, wash the bowl with clean, cold water and say a blessing over it before putting it away until next time.

Element: Earth

Cardinal Direction: North

Color: Black

Alchemic Shape: An inverted triangle with a line through the top section

Pillar: Silence

Earth is the base of nature. It represents solidity and tangible strength. Earth elements may seem less flashy than the others, but they are reliable and secure. Think of the amazing things that spring from the Earth; plants and flowers, foodstuff, and trees are all around you, but what else does the earth yield? Think about the diamonds and other Earth fortune-telling forms on the Earth.

Think of the Earth element as the Higgs Boson of your witchcraft; it brings the matter to your intent and makes it a tangible object. It is a healing element and works in spells that connect you to the essence of nature. Ancient civilizations created gardens and stone circles to channel the earth's energy (think Stonehenge or Machu Picchu) so you could create the same effect in your home.

The Earth Healing Mandala

Buddhists created mandalas to represent the universe – but in this example, you are creating a connection to the Earth. Choose a square box or garden planter and fill it with soil and sand. Choose a selection of white seeds and plant them in the corners to represent the four corners of creation. Now use a selection of colored seeds and grains to create a geometric pattern in the box. You can choose whatever pattern you like and whatever representation you desire. Be creative and energized, and fill the experience with joy.

You can chant and sing as you plant the seeds and maybe plant some in the moonlight to bring lunar energy. Let your inner voice guide you and show you the pattern in your mind. Once you have completed the mandala, leave it to root for seven days before you replant the seeds in your garden. The process can be repeated as many times as you like to spread the magic and bring the energy of Earth to your life.

Earth Protection Spell for the Home

Use Earth connections to make your home safe and free from attack by negative forces.

What You Need:

- 4 different dried herbs, cinnamon, black cohosh, tea, and cloves, work
- 4 black stones
- 4 natural pieces of wood, branches that have fallen, or driftwood

Bless all the items with the following words

"Mother Earth and sacred ground, here to stay, the magic is bound, to protect my home and keep it safe. Within these items, power is bound; by our reverence, our wounds will heal, and with these words, the magic is sealed."

Use the items to create a safe space around your home and form a barrier to all evil and negativity. You can repeat the words as many times as you like.

These are the traditional four elements of witchcraft and will help you become a more effective witch. The next two elements are less physical and more ethereal but are just as important in magic.

The Element of Self or Spirit

This element is non-physical and represents the connection between all things. It connects us to the universe and increases our awareness of the otherworldly magic.

It is represented by the colors white, violet, and black.

In magic, the crystal quartz brings the energy of spirit, and the number 1 is the corresponding number.

Its corresponding shape is a circle or spiral representing the power of the cycle of nature.

The fifth element isn't a modern concept. Aristotle and Plato began to debate the existence of a missing non-physical element, and they felt something was missing from the equation. They coined the element "*Aether*," which has become part of our language as "ether." The spirit element has no form and is pure energy, and invoking the spirit element is a powerful way to make your spells more potent.

How to Invoke the Spirit Element

Most practitioners use deities to invoke the spirit element, but others use spirit guides. There are six steps to invoking the element and summoning the energy to your world.

1. **Determine the spell or ritual you are going to perform.** The spirits need to know what energy to bring. Are you casting for love, financial gain, or protection? Be clear with your requirements and give as many details as you can. Setting your intention is crucial to success, so don't rush the process.
2. **Choose a spirit that suits your needs.** What energy does your spell need? Do you have connections to your spirit guides and ancestors? This topic will be covered later in the book, so you will better understand the available energy.
3. **Choose a time.** Timing is everything, and depending on your beliefs, you should plan to craft at a time when you feel most powerful and connected to the universe. If you work better with lunar energy, plan to craft at night. If you feel an affinity to certain astrological forces, check charts to choose an effective time for your work.
4. **Cleanse yourself.** This is an important part of the process. Use your regular cleansing ritual to dispel all the negative

energies and physical dirt from your body. Once you are cleansed, dress for the occasion in clean white clothes so your whole ethos sets your intention.

5. **Plan your words.** Write down your invocation and use positive and uplifting words. Say them clearly and with energy so the spirits know your intentions are true.

6. **Thank the spirits for their attention.** You should repeat the invocation as many times as needed, and you will know when the ritual has worked. After the intention is met, thank the spirits for their love and energy and meditate to regain your connection to the physical world.

And finally, the sixth element. Read on.

The Element of the Void

This element is the witchcraft version of the big bang theory. The dark void from which everything came. In magical terms, it is the starting pistol that signals the beginning of the race. It brings energy and intent to manifestation and acknowledges the power of the void.

There are several ways to bring the element of void to your craft. You can symbolize its presence with a black candle or an empty black vessel on your altar or directly invoke the element with a chant.

Chant to Invoke the Void

"I call upon the dark and formless part of the universe that gave birth to the eternal energy to bring itself to my work. I stand at the crossroads of magic and potentiality and ask that my words create success. As I speak, so may it be!"

These six elements are your keystones for witchcraft and will be there for you when needed. Remind yourself of their power by placing a pentagram close to your altar. The five points represent the first five elements, and the spaces remind you of the void.

Chapter 4: Gods and Goddesses in Witchcraft

Many witches choose to work with higher powers to assist them in their craft. They use these connections just like friendships in regular life and often have deities related to or associated with different religions and beliefs. Just like regular friendships, you need to understand the characteristics of these deities and how they work. With this knowledge, you can choose deities that suit your personality and beliefs - those which work with you at a pace that suits both of you. Choosing these deities and powers is as important as choosing the right tools or herbs to suit your magic.

Let's start with Wiccan deities. Wiccans are generally polytheists, meaning they worship more than one deity and invoke many gods and goddesses to bring them closer to the divine spirit of the universe. In Wiccan beliefs, the divine spirit is the very center of their magic, and all paths lead to this ultimate source.

The divine spirit is incomprehensible to human conception. Wiccans use deities to filter the divine spirit into traits and characteristics that we can understand. They all represent certain aspects of the spirit that help you form a bigger picture and better understand the divine spirit and what it means.

The Wiccan Triple Goddess

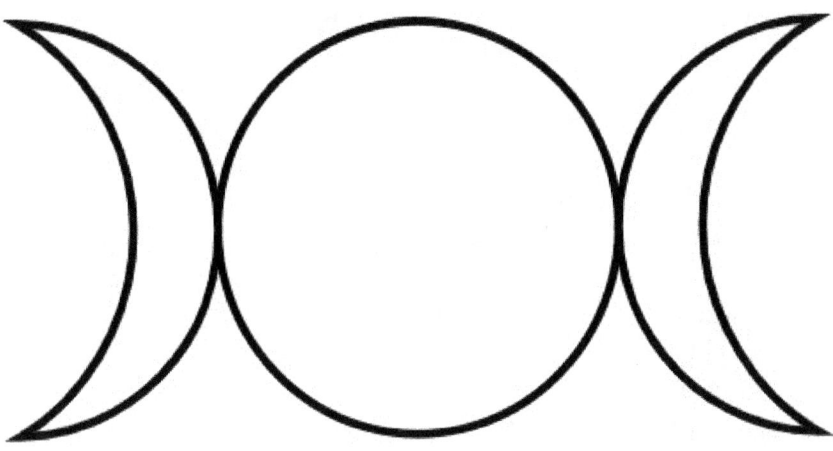

The symbol represents the three cycles of womanhood, the maiden, the mother, and the crone.'

The symbol of the triple goddess is a full moon accompanied by the waxing and waning moon. The goddess has three separate identities, and they represent the three cycles of womanhood. The maiden, the mother, and the crone are the three representations of femininity.

The Maiden

The beautiful young woman who is just starting to live her adult life. She represents the opportunities of life and the start of new beginnings. Witches call upon the maiden in spells for purification and blessings.

The Mother

At this stage, the goddess has become the embodiment of womanhood, and she is the symbol of fertility and life. The goddess is called upon in rituals that bless children or promote fertility, and she is also called upon to give guidance and wisdom. Wiccans believe that this stage of the goddess is just as important as their real mother.

The Crone

In regular society, older ladies are often associated with frailty and weakness, but Wiccans believe otherwise. They recognize the importance of experience and wisdom and will call upon the crone to bring knowledge from the spiritual world. Wiccans believe that the crone is the height of her power, and she is the source of everlasting power and psychic development.

The Horned God

While the triple goddess is the feminine representation of Wicca, the male counterpart is the horned god. He is strongly connected to the underworld and is often invoked in funeral rites and communicating with the dead. The horned god has antlers and can seem scary and evil, but he is a benevolent deity who acts as a guide and protector. Death is a normal part of life, and Wiccans embrace this and use the horned god to guide them to the underworld.

Some people connect the horned god to the Christian concept of the devil, but this is a false connection. The horned god was worshiped by the Pagans way before the era of Christianity, and he predates the Devil by centuries. He is a protector, represents the omnipotent father figure, and is a power of nature.

The Wiccan Lord and Lady

Symbolized by the female aspect of the sun and the male energy of the moon, the lord and lady are representatives of the duality of nature. They symbolize how male and female energies combine to create magic. In Wiccan ceremonies, the high priest and priestess will often adopt the roles of the lord and lady.

The One

Technically not a deity, The One is more like a cosmic ocean where every living and spiritual thing originated. Wiccans believe that all life comes from The One and don't invoke it or worship it like a deity. Instead, they use the energy from The One to inspire their work and create more effective magic.

Gods and Goddesses for Witchcraft

Sometimes, choosing certain deities to work with can be challenging and overwhelming. There are so many religions and belief systems to choose from that it is difficult to know where to start. The list below will help you start the process and connect you to some of the more approachable deities used by witches and other magical practitioners.

Adonis and Aphrodite – The original power couple who are powerful Greek deities. They can help you with spells for love and passion, bringing purity to your spellcasting.

Adonis and Aphrodite.[5]

Artemis and Apollo - Twin sister deities that work well in lunar magic.

Artemis and Apollo.[6]

Athena – The Greek goddess of hunting brings strength and courage to your craft.

Athena, goddess of hunting.⁷

Bast – The Egyptian goddess of cats and a source of feline wiles and knowledge.

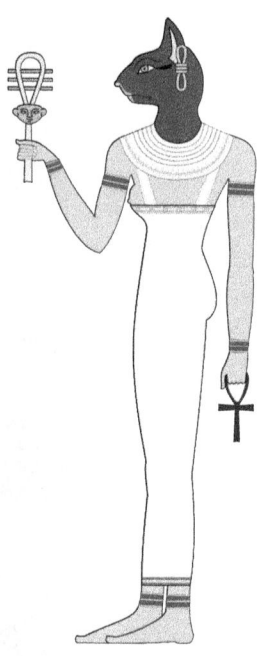

Bast, goddess of cats.⁸

Belenus or Bel – The Gaullist god of light and the sun, this Celtic god is often depicted with his horse and has powers related to equine strengths.

Bel, god of light and the sun.'

Brigid – The Celtic goddess of fertility and inspiration, invoked for fertility rites and the blessing of children.

Brigid, goddess of fertility and inspiration.[10]

Cerridwen – Welsh goddess of the moon and harvest; she brings abundance and prosperity to magic.

Cerridwen, goddess of the moon and harvest.[11]

Cernunnos – Celtic god of fertility and nature. He represents the underworld and is often pictured with horns and hooves.

Cybele – The Greek goddess of natural cavers who is especially effective in spells and rituals performed in nature, especially mountain tops and caves.

Demeter – The Greek goddess of fruitfulness. She brings good luck, prosperity, and abundance, especially to spells and rituals for crops and agriculture.

Diana – The Roman goddess of the hunt. Diana is a powerful female deity and brings courage, endeavor, and love to magic.

Dryads - A collection of tree spirits that are featured in Greek mythology. They are female representations of free spirit and playfulness. They bring lightness and joy to your magic.

Dryads.[13]

Flora - The Roman goddess of spring. Her energy is often used in rebirth magic and spells for new beginnings. She is a young and vibrant goddess who is filled with love and joy.

Fortuna - The Roman goddess of fate. Invoke her when you are performing divination or want to see what the future holds for you. She is a benevolent spirit who will work with you to change your fate and improve your future.

Freya - Also known as Frigg, is the Norse goddess from Asatru belief who is the consort of Odin and the leader of the Valkyries. She rules as the Queen of Asgard and the foremost goddess of Norse beliefs.

Hathor - The Egyptian goddess of the sky. She is especially effective in magic that is performed by females. Her protective energy is used to keep women safe and brings fertility and safety to them. She is often portrayed as a female form with a cow's head.

Hera - The wife of Zeus, Hera is the Greek goddess of marriage and relationships. She is one of the most effective goddesses of Greek mythology and can be invoked to bring feminine energy.

Hestia – The Greek goddess of home and hearth. Invoke her when you perform spells and rituals in your home to protect you from invasive energies.

Inanna – The Sumerian goddess of Heaven and divine law. She is a powerful sexual force and is especially effective in matters of love and law.

Isis – The Egyptian equivalent of the triple goddess of Wicca. She has the same three stages as the triple goddess.

Janus – The Roman God of entrances and transitions. He is especially effective in spells for new beginnings and guarding your emotional balance.

Kali – The consort of Shiva and a powerful source of both destruction and creation. Invoke her to banish your enemies or to help you start new activities.

Kali, the consort of Shiva and a powerful source of both destruction and creation.[18]

Mayet – The Egyptian goddess of justice, truth, and legal matters.

Morrigan – The Celtic equivalent of the triple goddess, strongly associated with death and war. She is depicted as a crow and has dark magical powers.

Muses – In Greek mythology, the Muses are goddesses of literature, science, and the arts. There are nine muses, and they can be invoked as a spiritual team to help your magic be more effective.

Nike – The Greek goddess of victory. Her power is effective to magic devoted to speed and success. She is often depicted with wings and is an effective symbol of art and sports.

Norns – In Norse mythology, the Norns are the sacred guardians of the tree of life, Yggdrasil, and they are effective protectors and control the fate of all human beings. They draw water from the well of creation to feed the sacred tree and are powerful female spiritual entities.

Norns: sacred guardians of the Tree of Life.[14]

Nut - The Egyptian goddess of the skies and the mistress of protection. She is depicted on all fours covering the Earth and protecting humankind.

Persephone - The Greek goddess of the underworld. Invoke her to help you cope with grief and guide your loved ones to the afterlife.

Selene - The Greek goddess of the moon.

Venus - The Roman goddess of love who is especially powerful in spells for love, lust, passion, and relationships.

Vesta - The Roman goddess of fire, both domestic and ritualistic.

How to Invoke or Evoke the Gods and Goddesses

One common witchcraft question is about invoking and evoking deities. Because the words sound similar, some beginners think the two practices are interchangeable when, in reality, the opposite is true. When you start working with deities, you must be extra careful and understand exactly what you are working with.

Evoking is the practice of asking a deity to join you during a ritual or working spell so you can benefit from their wisdom or energy. Any involvement is external and cannot harm you. Evoking can be achieved by a simple question or offering. For instance,

> *"Hail Venus, I ask you to join my sacred circle tonight and be part of my ritual for love and passion; we bring you this goblet of wine to show our love and respect."*

Then you hope the goddess hears your plea and joins you for your spell.

Invoking is a form of voluntary possession where the deity will manifest through your human form. This is much more involved than hanging out with your favorite deities and should only be performed by experienced witches. While the possession is always temporary, it is a good idea for beginners to practice evoking before they jump straight into invoking.

The Commonsense Guide to Invoking Deities

Once you feel ready to work with the deities, it is important to understand what preparation you need to do. Don't try and work with more than four deities when you first start, you need to get to know them, and they need to get to know you as well. The point is to be respectful and honorable and to build a relationship between both parties, so choosing too many deities could be confusing.

Other Preparations to Carry Out Before Invoking a Deity

- **Research and study your chosen deity.** Understand the myths in which they feature and their characteristics and personalities. What are their strengths, and what will they bring to your life?
- **Find appropriate ways to welcome your deity.** What adornments should you use to welcome them to your space? Appropriate symbols and figures from their cultural beliefs.
- **Choose suitable offerings** and libations for your chosen deity.
- **What are their favored animals or sacred items** which feature in their myths?
- **Document and research** any spells or rituals that are personal to the deity.
- **Look within your psyche** and be honest about the connection you feel to the deity.

The last point is the most important one. You need to feel a real connection and desire to work with your chosen deity. Sacred beings aren't in the market for casual relationships, and they will not respond to a halfhearted *"Hi, how are you"* because they are busy. Are you choosing this particular deity for the right reasons or just because they are cool and popular? The sacred beings you are invoking are serious about what they do and will only reply to people who are on the same wavelength as them.

Another thing to remember is that they are in charge. You could end up in a call-waiting system if your deity is busy, waiting a long time for an answer – only to be told no. That is the way of the universe when it comes to new energies; you may have to try multiple times before you achieve connection.

Why would you do all that preparation? Ask yourself if you would randomly walk up to a stranger in the street and ask them for help. Would you knock on a stranger's door and ask them to be part of your life?

It's a bit rude, not to say downright dangerous, and it just wouldn't happen. Magic isn't careless; you shouldn't cut corners because the whole process could spiral out of control. Good intentions aren't enough; you need to be thorough and respectful of the powers you are dealing with.

Ritual to Invoke a God or Goddess

Now you are ready to start the process. You have your chosen deity, are sure about your intent, and are mentally and physically ready to connect. What do you do next?

First, you must cleanse yourself spiritually and physically. Take a ritual bath with cleansing herbs and sea salt and let yourself dry naturally, don't rush the process using towels. Meditate before you start the ritual and dress in simple white cotton clothes.

Now you must ask for protection. Ask the spirits to keep you safe, and imagine a bright white light surrounding you as you feel their love and warmth. Now your body is protected, it's time to make a sacred space for your invoking ritual and spell. Take 40 candles and place them in a circle all around you. Sit in the middle of the circle and say the following:

> *"As I appear before you, almighty spirit, I ask for the wisdom to understand you. Give me access to your realm and grant me a safe passage to the inner domain. I ask for permission to enter your plane and connect to my chosen deity."*

You will feel different when you are given access and immediately feel lighter and more incisive. You could start to see images from the spiritual realm and feel the air around you change. Once you have stepped over the threshold, your energy levels will soar, and you can start to look for the answers you seek.

The next part of the invocation is incredibly personal, and the only advice you need is to follow your instinct and become immersed in the experience. Use your sincerity and love for the deities to connect with them. No formal words cover this connection; the words you use will come to you and will originate from your desire and need for their assistance.

Once you have connected to the deities and spirits, it's time to end the ritual. Thank the deities and spirits for their time and assistance, and cooperation. Be grateful for the answers you have received, and don't worry if all your queries haven't been answered. This starts a lifelong relationship with the divine universe and the higher beings occupying it.

How to Cast an Invocation Spell

This is a spell that can be used to draw spirits, deities, gods, and goddesses. It opens the lines between you and the spirit world. Cast this spell on a Wednesday during a full or dark moon for the best results.

What You Need:

- An offering for the deity – use your research to find out what is appropriate
- Silver candle (white will do if you don't have a silver one)
- Sage smudge stick
- 1 cup of sea salt

Prepare for the spell just as you would for the ritual by bathing and dressing in white. Cast your protection circle in salt and call the cardinal quarters for added protection. Light the smudge stick and use it to cleanse the area and yourself, then leave it burning in the circle. Take the candle and a holder and place them in the center of the circle while surrounding it with the gifts you have for the deity. Close your eyes and breathe deeply before you say the following:

"I call on you (insert deity name) and wait for you with an open mind and a grateful heart,

(Deities name) I call on you with an open mind and willing spirit,

(Deities name) I offer these gifts to honor you and make you feel welcome in my world,

Visit me and share your wisdom and knowledge and guide me through my craft."

When you feel the spell has finished, thank the deity for their attention and let the candle burn away naturally. Over the next few days, you will feel the sense of the deity's energy in your body, and you will hear voices and see images that originate from the deity's energy.

The bottom line is to trust your instincts and follow the path you are shown. Your regular senses are redundant in magic, and you need to call on your gut reaction and believe what you are being told. Use your mind and emotions to guide you and give yourself to the process.

Chapter 5: Tarot Cards

Tarot cards are a path to revealing the lessons of life.[16]

In the past, tarot cards were dismissed as hokey, and the image of a dodgy fortune teller earning money from saps who wanted to know what their future held was a popular misconception. Today users know better. The tarot card readings are so much more than divination and fortune-telling over-represent, respectively. They are a map of your soul and a way to see the story of your life. Some people see tarot as images on a deck of cards with defined meanings and as just a bit of fun. True believers know it is a path to revealing the lessons of life and a key to tapping into universal wisdom to gain knowledge.

Tarot is a powerful tool to expand your consciousness and become more self-aware. Ask questions and get answers that reflect the wisdom of the universe intertwined with your powerful consciousness.

A Brief History of Tarot

The oldest tarot cards are believed to have been used in 1440 AD and were created for the Duke of Milan. It is thought they were originally used to play a game rather than tell fortunes, and they were hand painted and ornate.

The game quickly spread to the rest of Europe and became a staple of rich households. This continued for the next 300 years when occult practitioners used them as a divination tool. The images were linked to ancient Egyptian lore, astrology, and alternative illustrated cards. The deck developed into the tarot cards known today in the 1970s when a growing interest in psychoanalysis linked the cards' meanings to science.

The New Age movement of the 1970s meant that popular culture and beliefs spread the use of tarot, and the interest grew. Today there are thousands of decks to choose from, and tarot is becoming a primary way to meditate and reflect on your personal state of being. The cards can be used to create a life plan to what you already know and what the cards can tell you.

How to Choose Your First Tarot Deck

First, let's get rid of the biggest misconception about tarot decks. There is a superstition that your first deck should never be bought by yourself; instead, it should be a gift from someone else. This is rubbish and an old wife's tale. Getting your first deck is exciting, but it can be overwhelming. There are so many decks to choose from, so here are some tips to help you get started on your journey.

- Explore the imagery of the decks and use your gut feeling to guide you.
- Remember to choose your deck depending on your experience level; beginners' cards are easier to use and can ease you into the process.

- Do you want to use traditional or more modern decks?
- Where are you going to use the cards?
- Is the size appropriate and practical?
- Choose a quality deck depending on your budget.

If you are eager to get started, printable decks are available online. These give you a chance to start your tarot journey in minutes.

Familiarize Yourself with the Deck

All decks have 78 cards, and these are divided into 2 major groups.

The Major Arcana has 22 cards, starting with the Fool tarot card, number 0, and running through to the World tarot card, numbered 21. They work together to form a story known as the Fool's Journey, during which lessons can be learned from each archetype within the Major Arcana.

The Minor Arcana contains the rest of the cards and contain 4 suits of 14 cards each. These are the Cups, the Pentacles, Swords, and Wands.

The Suit of Cups

All the cards in this suit are related to the element of water and are related to matters of the heart. Cards from this suit show emotional connections and how you are dealing with your environment.

The Suit of Pentacles

All the cards in this suit relate to the earth element. These are also known as money cards and deal with your prosperity and achievements. They answer questions regarding your career, money-related decisions, and financial matters. It is just as important to get answers to material-based questions as it is to deal with emotional matters.

The Suit of Swords

All the cards in this suit relate to the element of air. These cards tell you about communication and action. The cards will appear in a reading when you need to be reminded to use your head rather than your heart. If you receive a card of Swords, you should pay attention to your environment and beware of conflict and arguments that are brewing beneath the surface.

The Suit of Wands

These cards are related to the element of fire. They represent passion and inspiration and indicate the need to get creative and start new projects. These cards add heat to your life and bring a burst of energy that inspires you to do better. They encourage you to examine your core beliefs and to follow a path that suits your need. Wand cards aren't passive. They are firecrackers that are designed to light your internal fires.

This is just the start of your understanding of tarot and what the cards are trying to tell you. The information above is like a basic alphabet, and learning tarot is just like learning a new language. All the cards have multiple meanings, and the meanings change depending on the other cards in a spread. Each card represents individual words, and when used together, they begin to form sentences. It's just like when you begin to speak a new language, and you start to recognize the nuances and inflections that can influence the meaning and change the mood of the message.

How to Understand Your Deck

As a beginner, it is tempting to choose multi-card spreads, but that is not the right way to start understanding your cards. Beginners need to learn how to walk before they can run, and this involves pulling a single card daily and following the steps below:

1. Think of your question. What is the main thing bothering you, or do you have a practical question you need to answer?
2. Close your eyes and visualize your question, how the different answers can manifest, and what can happen with multiple outcomes.
3. Open your eyes and pull a card from your deck.
4. Study the card at length.

Which card did you get, and from which part of the deck did it come? Use the information above to get the basic meaning of your card.

Study the imagery and look beyond the picture to see any hidden meaning. Are there any other cards you would like to see alongside your card? What would it mean in a conventional spread? If you pull your card in the morning, carry it with you for the rest of the day so you can feel its presence. Take the card out, study it whenever possible, and see if your feelings change as the day progresses.

At night, sleep with the card under your pillow and see what dreams you have. Are they related to the card and your perceived meanings, or are they completely different? Are your dreams telling you to change your perception, or are they confirming your initial thoughts? The following day you should start seeing signs related to the card and connecting the message. Over time you will realize that these things aren't happening by coincidence.

Repeat the process until you feel you have a deeper understanding of the deck and what the cards mean. You will instinctively know when to start using spreads instead of single cards and let the cards work to create stories for you.

Popular Spreads for Beginners and Advanced Users

You already know that tarot is based on instincts, but it is also influenced by the data you receive and how it is obtained. Choosing a pattern to represent your spread is the first step to triggering the process. This chapter deals with readings for yourself rather than other people, as this is the classic way to start your journey. You should never do readings for anyone else until you feel you have reached an expert level.

The Classic Three-Card Spread

You are both the reader and the querent in this reading, so you pose and answer the questions. The most common three-card spread involves the past, the present, and the future and begins with the first card setting the intent and theme of the answer that is being indicated.

The second card sets the nature of the question and the current position of your emotions or practical situation. It is placed alongside the first card before the third is pulled. This third card suggests the likely outcome and what the future looks like.

Once the three cards are in place, use your intuition to decipher the meaning and what your question is really about.

The Mind, Body, and Spirit three-card spread does the same as the past, present, and future spread but is more focused on adding balance to a reading. The first card represents the current state, the second is the approaching energies, and the third is advice for each realm.

The Five-Card Spread

This extends the three-card spread to include even more information and adds extra levels to the answers you can find. Five card tarot spreads help you get to the heart of the matter.

The spread should form a cross with the three original past, present and future cards forming the crosspiece. The other two cards are placed by the side to form the cross. The central three cards show the potential, while the additional cards indicate the brightest and darkest possibilities of the situation.

The Rectangle

Pull the first card from the deck and place it on the table. This is the theme card for the other four to relate to. Place it at the center and pull four additional cards to form a rectangle around the main card. The four cards represent the tools to be used, a lesson to be learned, another person's perspective, and any potential conflict or fears.

The Celtic Cross Spread

This spread uses ten cards and is an extension of the five-card spread. The first card represents your role in the question, and the second card is an obstacle you will face to reveal the answer. The second card crosses the first one and forms the center of the cross.

The third cross represents the foundation of the question that lies in the past. The fourth card is placed on the left side of the cross and represents an event that is happening in the present that is affecting the issue.

The fifth card is drawn and placed above the cross to represent the potential for success and a favorable outcome, while the sixth is something that will happen in the future that will bring about an outcome.

Once the cross has been formed, it's time to add four extra cards representing four more pieces of information that help address the issue.

Card 7 is related to past experiences and attitudes that may be affecting the theme of the question.

Card 8 is about external forces and their influence on the issue. Are there negative energies at work, or could the people around you make a difference in how you handle the issue?

Card 9 represents what your fears and hopes are. They will show you your subconscious feelings about issues, some of which have been hidden from sight.

Card 10 represents the probable outcome. It gives you the chance to accept your fate or do something to change it.

This is quite an advanced spread and can be confusing for beginners. Just like any other skill or gift, the more you practice, the better you will become. Just like learning a new language, tarot reading is an everlasting process, and you will learn more every time you use them.

FAQs about Tarot

Q1. Do I need to be psychic to read tarot cards?

No. You need to learn to trust your intuition and interpretation of the cards to guide you and read effectively. Of course, some people will have natural psychic abilities, which means that they are more effective than others, but it isn't essential to be psychic to read the cards.

Q2. Can anyone learn how to read tarot?

Yes, they can. Like the question above and just like regular life, some people will be more in tune with the cards and will have a natural affinity with them, but with practice and dedication, anyone can learn to read the cards.

Q3. Do you need intuition to read tarot cards?

Some people rely on their cards to give them a clear reading purely from the spread and the questions they are answering. This can lead to a dry reading without any wiggle room, but if you factor in intuition, you get a more effective and reliable reading that gives you a deeper connection to the cards.

Q4. Is my intuition fallible?

Just like all your instincts, intuition can lead you astray and down the wrong path. Even expert readers can be fooled by the signs and symbols the cards are showing and give the wrong reading. It's important to know that even though your intuition is critical for your readings, it isn't infallible and may be wrong.

Q5. Can tarot cards be used for fortune-telling?

No. They offer guidance and insight, but they should never be relied on to give you advice that changes your life. If you need professional advice, then seek it out. It's okay to ask the tarot cards for their take on things but always trust the professionals in certain matters. The cards can give you an insight into the future and the influences at play, but they aren't a predictive tool.

Tarot can be an exciting and powerful way to use your intuition to work with magic. It is a truly magical way to connect to the universe and your inner self. This is just a quick look at tarot, and if you feel a connection to the cards, you could be starting a lifelong relationship with your deck.

Chapter 6: Runic Divination

Runic symbols are believed to hold the keys to knowledge, wisdom, and spiritual power.[16]

Norse and Germanic folklore were filled with magic and witchcraft, and the existence of runes and their divination powers are rooted in their history. The Elder Futhark runes are the most famous runes from history, and they originated in the 2nd century and were used for six centuries after. The alphabet was 24 characters long and was often carved into stones and wooden tiles. As with most languages and forms of communication, the alphabet was subject to change, and by the 8th century, it had been whittled down to a 16-character form of runes known as the Younger Futhark runes.

The runes were used as a form of writing, and Norse people would use them to create texts, but the gods and the Norns (the Norse fates) believed they were more magical than that and used them to write on Yggdrasil, the Norse tree of life. They were used to tell tales of the destinies of men and the powers of the gods and were considered magical and powerful ways to tell the future.

Odin taught the Norse people how to use the runes to practice divination and use magical symbols to protect their homes and weapons. Swords and shields from the Norse era would have runes engraved on them to ensure the Viking warrior who carried them would be safe. The use of magical symbols was widespread and began to include more symbols from mythology, like the Norse Compass and the Helm of Awe, but the main decorations were based on the runes.

The practice of divination with runes isn't clear because of the lack of written evidence, and most of the information about runic use is gathered from the Roman historian Tacitus who wrote about Viking life. It is believed that the runes would be carved on small objects like bones and sticks, and the runemaster would then use them to cast a reading. Most of the evidence suggests that runemasters would often be women, and they were regarded as the wise keepers of the runes. They would ask a question and then cast the runes onto a sacred space to gain an insight into the future, depending on where the runes fell. However, because of the lack of evidence, that is all that is known about the practice.

Modern Runic Divination

The advance of Christianity and the Latin language meant that runes were assigned to history for a long time. They were used by some isolated Scandinavian communities and are still used by them today. The re-emergence of runic magic began in the 17th century when a Swedish mystic associated with the emerging Kabbalah Jewish tradition was inspired to use runes for divination purposes. He was visited by spirits who sent him visions to inspire the use of the Younger Futhark runes in practice.

Some modern runemasters still use the Futhark runes, but the majority have adopted the Armanen runes created at the beginning of the 1900s by the Austrian occultist Guido von List. He based his runes on the earlier symbols. Still, over the last hundred years, they have also been adapted and changed to suit modern language. The symbols and their meanings must reflect matters of the era, so the more modern interpretations account for this.

Meanings of Runes

As already discussed, the meanings have their roots in Norse mythology and have been changed to suit modern needs. Still, many runemasters will incorporate both in their readings. Like tarot, runes have multiple interpretations based on how they fall and which other runes accompany them. The practice is based on intuition and what you see in the runes, but the meanings below will help you learn how to read the runes and adapt your thinking.

The table below lists the runes with their English phonetic form, how to pronounce them, and the meaning of the rune:

F - Frey - Wealth and riches

Frey, represents wealth and riches.[17]

U - Ur - Rain, snow precipitation

Ur, represents rain, snow, and precipitation.[18]

Th - Thur - Giant, dangerous, emotional distress

Thur, represents giant, dangerous, and emotional distress.[19]

A - As - The Morse God Odin, wetlands, the kingdom of heaven

As represents the Norse god Odin, wetlands, and the kingdom of heaven.[20]

R - Reed - Ride, speed, travel, journey

200-450 AD   450-550 AD   550-750 AD

Reed, represents a ride, speed, travel, and journey.[21]

K - Kan - Death, illness, cancer, abscess

Kan represents death and illness.[22]

H - **Hagal** - Passageways, frost, cold

Hagal represents the cold.[33]

N - **Naudr** - Desire, need, barriers, obstacles

Naudr represents desire, need, barriers, and obstacles.[34]

I - **Isa** - Icicles, destruction, extreme cold

Isa represents icicles, destruction, and extreme cold.[35]

A - **Arr** - Abundance, harvesting, times of plenty

Arr represents abundance.[36]

S – Sol – Solar energy, sun, warmth, heat

Sol represents solar energy, sun, warmth, and heat.²⁷

T – Tur – Justice, law, fairness

Tur represents justice, law, and fairness.²⁸

B – Bjork – New beginnings, springtime, the birch tree

Bjork represents new beginnings, springtime, and the birch tree.²⁹

M - Madur - Humankind, man, male energy

Madur represents humankind, man, and male energy.[80]

I - Logur - Liquids, water, nature, waterfalls

Logur represents liquids, water, nature, and waterfalls.[81]

R - Yur - The yew tree, strength, tolerance, stamina

Yur represents the yew tree, strength, tolerance, and stamina.[82]

Do You Believe in Divination?

Back in Viking times, it was hard to conceive how many people believed in the process and how many believed in fate. Nordic folklore is filled with choices, and Asatru's religion is unique because *their gods were not worshiped.* Asatru followers believed their deities were prone to human frailties and would make mistakes just as humans do. The stories of the gods and goddesses are filled with incidents of them being tricked and fooled by mortals and other lesser beings.

It is important to recognize how modern rune readings work and what they can and can't tell you. Casting these magical symbols is fun and a great way to connect to magic, but it should never replace common sense and professional advice. Don't use reading to make life-changing decisions based on their answers. Instead, you should use the runes to help you get a better insight into what your subconscious is telling you and what the universe is suggesting. They are used to create a "divine spark" that connects you to the power of your mind, how you form an intrinsic part of the universe, and how everyone has a part to play. The difference between tarot and runes is the material used to create the runes. Tarot is highly personalized, while runes are made from physical materials that are part of the universe, like stones, glass, wood, and rocks.

Runes will often hint at an answer and show you the way to pursue the hints. The actual meaning of the word is whisper, secret, or mystery, depending on what you read. If your questions have multiple layers and need deeper introspection, then runes may be more effective than tarot, but the choice is yours. In Wiccan practices, runes are used to protect as well as to connect to the spiritual realm so you feel safer in your practices.

How to Choose Your Runes

Just like tarot decks, there are a lot of different rune sets to consider. There are ornate sets using materials like glass, crystal, and metal, and many simple sets are made from wood or stones. The material is your choice, and you may want to start with something simple to begin with. If you are naturally crafty, then consider making your own set from pebbles or wood. This way, you can start to feel a connection immediately, and your runes will be charged with your energy.

How to Store Your Runes

If you buy your runes, they will often come with a handy drawstring bag to keep them clean and safe. If you have made your own runes, you can buy pouches to store them or create a bag that suits your runes. They can also be kept in a box decorated with symbols and magical signs to keep their energy pure.

A rune cloth can be used to polish your set and keep it free from dust and negative energy. As a beginner, it can be a simple duster or a white cotton handkerchief, but as you start to form a relationship with your runes, you may want to choose something more personal. The cloth you choose can also be a base for your casting and create a boundary to keep negative energy out.

How to Get Started with Rune Casting

Choose a spot to cast that is familiar and brings you joy and peace. You must feel safe and relaxed, or your reading will be affected by stress. Take ten minutes to clear your mind and get rid of the detritus of regular life. Once you feel relaxed and ready to start, lay your rune cloth or board on the floor and start to think about the question you are asking. If you have connections with higher energies, call upon them to join you and guide your reading.

Just as with tarot, you should start with single runes to acquaint yourself with the set. Place your hand in the bag, draw your rune, and place it on the cloth or board. What does it say to you? What does it mean regarding your question? Focus on the single rune and what it is telling you.

Classic Rune Layouts and Casts

The Three Rune Layout

This simple cast is perfect for beginners and will help you start your journey with the runes. Reach into your bag and take the first rune out. Place it on your cloth or board with intent. This first rune should be right of center. Now draw the second rune and place it in the center before drawing the third to go to the left.

Rune 1 - This represents the overview of your situation or question. It is the rune's general opinion about what is happening and will help to set the scene.

Rune 2 - This represents the challenge and obstacles that lay before you.

Rune 3 - This represents the course of action and what you can do to get past these obstacles and be successful.

The Five Rune Layout

This extension of the three-rune layout includes more specific time periods. The first rune should be laid at the center of the cloth, while the four remaining runes form a cross around it. Rune 2 should be at the west point, 3 should be at the north, 4 at the south, and 5 should be at the east.

In this reading, the runes should be placed face down and turned over in order of placing to give a more effective reading. The horizontal runes 2, 1, and 5 represent the past, the present, and the future, while rune 4 represents the elements of the problem, and rune 3 relates to what you need to do to resolve the issue.

The Nine Rune Cast

This is for more experienced casters but gives you a more detailed and insightful answer to your questions. When using this casting method, you must fully delve into your spiritual learnings and prepare for the experience. You may want to directly connect to your spirit guides and ask for their guidance before you cast and ask them to join you in your reading. You can enhance your surroundings with magical tools and a candle or two. Dress for the occasion in simple white robes to make the reading feel more magical.

Of course, you can just cast your runes as normal in a quiet place that connects you to the universe. Divination is more achievable when you feel relaxed and comfortable, so your surroundings should reflect that. Some people may be more at home in a loud environment, while others prefer naturally calm surroundings. We are all different, and magic helps us celebrate that fact.

Reach into your bag and select nine runes at random. If your runes are large, then use both hands to choose them and then hold onto the runes for a moment or two. Now scatter the runes on your cloth or board while you look upwards. Consider the runes and how they have fallen. The ones near the center are considered the most important, while those on the periphery are less influential. If the runes are touching or very close, they could be complimentary runes that strengthen their influence. If the runes are face down, they should be left that way while you study the ones that have landed face up. Take a notebook and make a note of them so you can study them later before you turn over the remaining runes. Remember to place the runes you have turned over in exactly the same position they landed in so you get the overall picture when all nine runes are in place. The runes you have turned over represent the future and other outside influences that could affect your issues. They also represent the potential of new possibilities and future opportunities.

The Three Norns Cast

This is another simple cast based on the Norse divinities known as the Norns. The three principle Norns were sisters who lived beside the Well of Ur and created the fate of mankind. This rune cast represents the sisters and helps you see different aspects of your issue.

The first rune should be cast to represent the past and how it affects you. Do you have issues from your past that have followed you into your current life and are affecting you? The rune will highlight any historical issues.

The second rune gives you a deeper understanding of your issues and how they affect you.

The third rune is attuned to the future and will show you how to move forward.

There are hundreds of different casting layouts and ways to use the runes. Once again, you should use your intuition to guide you to the layouts that work for you.

Casting Boards

Some practitioners prefer to use a board decorated with Nordic symbols to bring further depth to their casts. These boards are similar to Ouija boards in some cases, with letters and numbers on them and a dedicated *Yes* and *No* area. Other boards concentrate on Nordic symbols like the Norse cosmos, which can represent the different areas of the Nordic universe. The central realm of Midgard represents the heart of the reading, while the inner realms of Asgard and Helheim represent the psychological influences. The outer realms of Jotunheim and Muspelheim are the unprejudiced areas of the universe.

The elements can also create a powerful runic board. Choose a board and divide it into four equal sections. Paint or color the sections white, red, blue, and green to represent respectively air, fire, water, and earth. Draw a magic circle in the center and decorate it with your favorite symbols and signs. When you want a detailed cast, simply scatter the whole bag of runes onto the board.

How each rune falls will tell you something different. Are they in the circle or outside? What color are they in, or do they land on the dividing line? What do the elements mean to you?

Air

Generally, air represents intelligence and creativity. It is the element of new beginnings, and if your rune falls in this section, it relates to your intangible issues and how to deal with them. This is the element of creativity and moving forward.

Fire

The element of passion and love fire can mean removing impurities and stopping harmful habits. Are there things holding you back? Burn them and move on. Fire is the symbol of transformation, and your rune will land there to signify your inner strength and the heat of your passion.

Water

Emotional and unconscious issues will be dealt with in this section. Water is one of the two physical elements and represents the ability to change and interact. Water fills spaces with ease and is considered a natural signal to become more adaptable and accept your situation.

Earth

The second physical element is less fluid than water and represents stability and foundation. Earth symbolizes fertility and material objects, and your rune will highlight what new beginnings you need to address. It is the element of stillness and endings, so your rune could tell you what part of your life has ended and how to move on.

The circle on the board could represent the other element we covered earlier, the element of spirit. If your rune falls within the circle, it could mean it is more personal and related to yourself, while outside the circle could mean it represents your environment.

Your runes and boards should represent your personality and beliefs. If you feel inspired by Disney characters or figures for literature, then use them to decorate your boards. There are no hard and fast rules to runic divination;. Your inspiration should be how you fuel your intuition, so be creative and create multiple sets to suit the situation. Runes and runic boards are by nature decorative, so use them to decorate your home or sacred space to bring color and protection.

Chapter 7: Crystal Divination

When you think of crystal divination, most people think of the crystal ball, a mystical gypsy woman in a booth at the fair, and tales about what will happen. Modern witches know that divination is all about connecting to your inner psyche and the universe, and they understand that one of the most effective materials to use is crystals. They are naturally incredible and represent some of nature's most beautiful aspects in their magnificence.

Crystals are powerful and beautiful, and your collection will clearly indicate how you work and connect to the universe. Have you ever noticed how some people look like their

Crystals represent some of nature's most beautiful aspects in their greatness.[38]

pets? Well, choosing a crystal is a bit like choosing a puppy. You should feel an immediate connection with it and be prepared to look after it, nurture it, and care for it as you would a child or pet.

Crystals to Enhance Divination

This list contains just a few suggestions and will help you choose your starter kit for divination purposes.

Apophyllite - This crystal is the keeper of the Akashic Records, the knowledge of what all lives will look like and what happens to each of us. This crystal helps you break the barrier between the physical and spiritual worlds and keeps the physical body safe during your astral travels. Use the apophyllite to help you with out-of-body experiences and astral traveling.

Apophyllite brings down the barrier between the physical and spiritual worlds.[84]

Amethyst - The third eye crystal and the representative of the crown and heart chakras. Because amethyst is so in tune with your higher chakras, it is the perfect choice for divination pendulums. Suspend the crystal from a chain and ask it questions with an answer board or by using left and right to indicate yes and no.

Aquamarine - A healthy clarifying stone, aquamarines are connected to the element water. They will help you focus and become more in tune with your psychic abilities.

Azurite - A crystal attuned with extremely high frequencies and gives you the power to enhance your third eye and higher crown chakras. Azurite is also used to make crystal elixirs for physical healing and energy readings. Soak the crystal in water to create an elixir to drink before you do tarot readings or crystal gazing so you increase your intuition and clairvoyance.

Azurite can improve your clairvoyance.[85]

Beryl –Golden beryl is a highly effective stone for scrying and other magic rituals.

Bloodstone – This crystal facilitates your clairaudience powers so you can hear the spirits clearly and understand their message. It also enhances dreaming and can make your nightly messages more distinct and direct.

Calcite – The crystal of astral traveling and out-of-body experience. Use it when you want to cross the veil and channel your higher purpose. Spirits connect to calcite and will use their energy to bring clearer and more detailed messages.

Carnelian – Aids clairvoyance and helps the living transition to the spirit world. Use it in divination spells to connect with your ancestors and receive their messages. Carnelian enhances your psychic abilities and develops your connections to your guides.

Calcite can help with out-of-body experiences.[86]

Celestite – Helps when you need to recall a dream that feels important but has become vague in your waking mind. Improves communication with the spiritual world and the higher energies.

Fluorite – The purple or violet form of fluorite improves your psychic connections and helps you decipher psychic messages. Use it in spells and rituals to get a clearer idea of what the spirits are trying to tell you.

Herkimer Diamond – Helps the user connect to spirit guides and collect information about their past lives. Aids clairvoyance and other psychic strengths.

Herkimer diamonds can help you connect to spirit guides.[87]

Iolite – Strengthens psychic abilities and can help users find their psychic on-button and activate their spiritual connections.

Jasper – Increases the quality of dreams and adds prophetic skills so the user can interpret signs and symbols from the spirit world.

Jasper increases the quality of dreams.[88]

Labradorite – If you want a starter stone to use in divination, choose this one. According to Eskimo legend, the famous natural phenomenon, the Northern Lights, were once trapped in rocks along the Canadian coast at a place called Labrador. A famous warrior was traveling in the region and recognized what was happening. He used his mystical spear to free the lights and restore them to the heavens. Because the lights had been trapped for so long, they left a beautiful mark on the stones, and these became the powerful crystal labradorite we know today. They are the most powerful stones for divination and will help all your senses and connections.

Lapis Lazuli – An important stone for protection and spiritual enhancement. It enhances your third eye chakra and brings increased psychic communication.

Lapis Lazuli is helpful for protection.[39]

Malachite – This crystal works as an effective partner for azurite; together, the crystals give extra strength and psychic intuition.

Merlinite – Aids traveling through past lives and gaining extra knowledge from former existences. Helps the user to find knowledge to help them become more ascended and developed.

Moonstone – Links the user to lunar energy and helps them to achieve heightened spiritual connections. Enhances lucid dreaming and astral travel with heightened intuition.

Obsidian – the multitude of colors in the crystal makes scrying more detailed and provides enhanced readings.

Opal – Traditionally an unlucky stone in divination, it helps the user induce visions from higher beings and increases intuition.

Opal increases intuition.⁴⁰

Quartz – Strengthens the crown chakra and boosts the third eye power meaning the user will experience stronger communication from the spirits and higher beings.

Sapphire – This gemstone brings different qualities depending on the color. Black is intuitive, while purple helps the user improve their dream recollections. Green sapphires increase psychic skills, and blue sapphires enhance the third eye chakra.

Sodalite – Increases psychic experiences and brings a deeper understanding of messages and visions.

Turquoise – This ancient stone has been used to bridge the veil between the physical and spiritual realms for thousands of years.

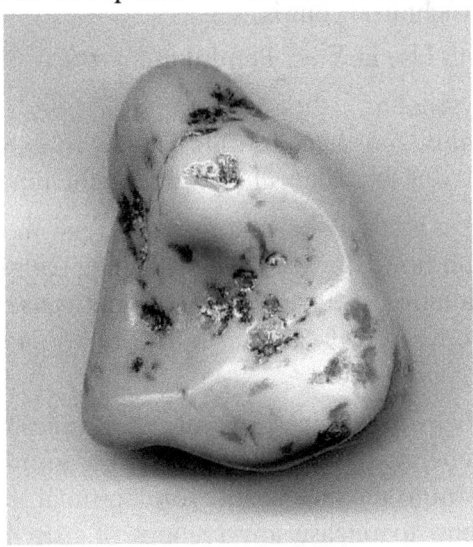
Turquoise can bridge the veil between the physical and spiritual realms.⁴¹

Crystals and How to Use Them in Divination, Healing, and Spiritual Awareness

Divination with crystals can be performed in many guises, and you can experiment to find the method that suits your style. Seers have been using crystals to foretell the future for generations, and the process is called lithomancy.

Pendulum Dowsing with Crystals

Back in ancient Egypt, Hindu cultures, and Chinese history, there are many records of crystal divination using pendulums. The crystals were attached to a chain and held at height to achieve vibrations that indicated the message from beyond. Some seers would calibrate their pendulum by setting clear instructions on what each movement indicates. Two nudges to the left for yes and two to the right for no are the first calibration.

Today, many practitioners use pendulum wheels to get clearer answers and more detailed readings. They create a wheel of possibilities which is divided into 18 sections of 20 degrees to create 18 different specifics for your questions. These can include any details you feel are relevant to the questions you have about spirits and how they answer.

The crystals used in the pendulum are specific for the metaphysical answers you require, so using the relevant crystal increases the chance of gaining effective insight into your issues.

Which Crystal to Use in Your Pendulum:

- Rose crystals are the best for questions about love and relationships. Ask the spirits about your soulmates and true love and what your love life will look like in the future.

- Amethyst crystals help you find answers about your spiritual destiny and how your past life is affecting your karmic debt. Use the pendulum to answer questions that cause you anxiety and fear so you can feel calmer and more connected to your past and future existences.

- Sodalite helps you improve your communication and deal with negative energy. They increase your communication skills and connect you to the angels and your spiritual team. Use them in a pendulum to release any feelings of hatred and jealousy to regain your spiritual balance.

- Labradorite is the crystal of the Aurora Borealis and helps you answer questions about your destiny. It represents the power of healing and dream therapy and will help you feel more grounded in times of chaos and crisis.
- Red jasper pendulums increase your sense of confidence and courage. Use it to ask the spirits to help you feel more able to resolve conflicts without harm and to bring peace to your life.
- Black tourmaline helps you feel protected and safe from psychic attacks. If you feel you are psychically blocked, use a black tourmaline pendulum to open those blocked chakras and resume all forms of spiritual connections.

Crystals for Scrying

Scrying is divination gained from looking into clear surfaces and seeing visions. Perhaps the most traditional method is the crystal ball which has already been mentioned. Still, modern practitioners know that many different crystals will serve the purpose without buying a ball. The crystals absorb and store energy from the universe and help you tune into your higher self and the spirit world to gain insight and knowledge.

Black obsidian is a natural choice for scrying. With its deep black color, it is an effective way to see images. Try scrying in the light of a new moon to get results and stare into the crystal at eye level while you meditate upon what you want the crystal to show you. The results should include clear images of which spirits and subconscious beliefs are right for you.

Quartz crystal is a clear option for scrying and gives you clarity of vision on its unflawed surface. Try scrying in low light, by candle perhaps, and invite the spirits to show you their answers and suggestions.

Polar jade crystals are a popular choice for divination because of the depth of clarity they provide. It has been referred to as "The Stone of Power" by healers and seekers for generations, and it is effective in protection and connection to your higher self. It has powerful healing qualities and is used to process insights and enhance concentration.

Smoky quartz is perfect for beginners as it is a calming and grounding crystal that absorbs negative energy. It will keep you safe and protected during your divination and help you connect to the spirits effectively.

Crystals for Clairvoyance

Iolite

Also known as the Viking's compass, iolite was a key part of the Vikings' discovery of the New World as it reduced glare and polarized sunlight so the Viking sailors could navigate more effectively. The element of air rules iolite, increasing its ability to unlock dormant skills and abilities, including clairvoyance. If you lie on the floor and place an iolite crystal on your forehead between the brows, it helps you to boost your concentration and improve your memory.

Iolite can also clear your mind of mental chatter and increase your capacity for learning while it also helps boost your energy levels. Use an elixir made from iolite crystals and water to fill yourself with solar energy and positivity.

Kyanite

These crystals help you improve your clairvoyance skills and balance all the chakras in the body. It will flush out toxins from them and help you reclaim your intuition and gain hereditary magic from your ancestors. Wear it on your body to increase spiritual communication throughout your regular life.

Labradorite

Once again, the versatile crystal of labradorite helps you achieve clairvoyance. It is especially effective in stimulating your brain and teaching it how to recognize signs from the spirits. It activates the throat and third eye chakras, which make clairvoyance more achievable.

Amazonite for Ghostly Divinations

If your interest is piqued by communicating with ghosts, then consider using Amazonite crystals, which open up other realms and protect you from evil. The main difference between ghosts and spirits is that ghosts are always the souls of deceased people, while spirits could have lived on Earth but not necessarily in human form. Ghosts will appear to you in human form and can often present as their human form, and they feel and act differently to spirits.

Ghosts are often tied to their location due to the tragic circumstances of their passing, and some won't even realize they have passed. They may have tragic backgrounds and vibrate with chaotic energy, but very few of them wish you any harm. They may be confused and wish to complete unfinished business before they leave for the other realm, so if you do contact them, be prepared for a sad story or even anger. This is a specialized form of divination that beginners should not undertake. Once you have become accomplished with spiritual communications, then you could try divination with ghosts and use Amazonite for your rituals.

Sodalite for Tarot Readings

If you do struggle to interpret the sign you are getting from your tarot cards, try putting a sodalite crystal by your table. It will help you connect to your inner wisdom and find meaning in the cards. Sodalite also reminds you to look deeper at your reasons for asking the questions and tap into your unused intuition.

Serpentine for Angelic and Otherworldly Connections

Serpentine is thought to be powered by the energy of the Greek Gorgon Medusa, the powerful guardian who could turn men to stone with just one glance. It is a powerful way to connect to other realms and find guidance from the angels and spirits that reside far beyond Earth. It will help you find your way if you are lost in your crafting, feeling uninspired, and at a loss to know what to do next.

Lapis Lazuli for Finding Your Tether

Sometimes magic and witchcraft can get overwhelming, and you feel like your spirit work and spellcasting have become stale and are going nowhere. Trust in lapis lazuli to help you find your roots and to create a tether in the spirit world. Sometimes there is so much activity it can be hard to identify your lead guardian, so ask lapis lazuli to help you with your search.

Divination may seem like a new age activity and is a fun way to collect shiny crystals, tarot cards, and runes, but the practice has its roots deeply entrenched in ancient cultures. Buddhism, pagan, Judaism, and Christianity all have records of wise men or seers using divination to look into the future. Today, it is known that a lot of reading is powered by the subconscious, powered by the energy of the universe or the spirit world. You don't have to be religious or be affiliated with a certain belief to practice divination. You just have to believe.

Keep yourself safe with the normal rules of witchcraft and always be respectful of the practice. The spirits are always ready to communicate with us providing we show them that we are involved for the right reasons. If you use divination for fun and trivial matters, tell them and ask if they will indulge you. The questions you ask don't always have to be life-changing; they just have to be honest and come from a place of love.

Chapter 8: Lunar Magic

Different phases of the sun and moon.⁴⁸

People take the moon and sun for granted. They know that both celestial bodies will be there every day, and the sun will bring warmth and light while the moon lights the night sky. It is impossible to imagine the world functioning without either, and that's because it wouldn't be able to.

Because of its magical properties, the moon is especially important and significantly affects how the Earth works and how humans feel emotionally. The power of lunar energy rules the tides and seas, and there is a reason why the word lunatic is used to describe a madman. Long ago, it was believed that humans behaved differently in the phases of the moon's cycle, and the same principles apply to magic. Every phase has the power to enhance your magic, providing you know how to use them.

Lunar magic is an archetype of magic, and the moon's powers have influenced mankind since time began. The moon has an incredible pull on mankind, and its cycles are intrinsic to magical powers. Most laypersons know the power of the full moon and what it brings to magic, but they are less aware of the properties of the other cycles. Witchcraft and magic will still work even if you aren't aware of which cycle the moon is in, but it is more likely to have more impressive results if you work with the moon and make sure the elements are all aligned for success. Just as in your regular life, the more resources you have available, the better the job gets done. It's worth delving into the different phases in-depth, but you may like to have a magical cheat sheet to start with. These simple breakdowns help remind you when to cast your spells and why. You can make them into reminders to keep by your altar or your magic tool store to use during your crafting.

The waxing moon is the time to:
- Draw money
- Attraction spells
- Progression and increasing spells
- Finding hidden talents
- Developing and pursuing new goals and skills

The full moon is the time to:
- Charge your crystals
- Work within a coven
- Work major spells
- Cast healing magic
- Raise power levels
- Wishing magic

The waning moon is the time to:
- Work on personal goals like weight loss
- Elimination spells
- Banishing magic
- Cleansing energies
- Moving on

The dark moon is the time for:
- Divination spells
- Consulting the oracle
- Starting new projects
- New beginnings
- Setting strong intentions

Magic for the Waxing Moon

This is the cycle of abundance, and like riding a wave inland, it makes things move more quickly and with more intention. This is the time to set spells for personal success and growth.

The spells below will give you a clear idea of how this cycle works, so go ahead and cast those spells for beauty and abundance. You deserve it.

Create a Plan for Personal Growth

On the first day of the waxing moon, start with a blank piece of paper and a pen. Write down what you plan to achieve and what outcomes would be best for you. Consider your relationship, your career, or your finances. What could improve these areas of your life? Now you have a blueprint for your success, and you can cast spells to perform rituals to make sure they happen. Start with a clear plan and prepare to celebrate your success when the full moon appears.

A Money Drawing Spell

What do your finances look like? Are you in debt, or would you simply like a bit more cash coming in? Use the waxing moon cycle to draw money into your life and create moneymaking opportunities.

Set out a place for you to sit in the moonlight on the first night of the waxing moon. Bring a green candle and a representative of money like a dollar bill or your wallet. Sit in meditation beneath the moonlight and say the following spell:

"Lunar power, come to me, bring me luck and wealth, fill my wallet and my life with abundance and love, and make it so."

Let the candle burn down naturally and bury the wax in the ground. When you have completed the spell, you will start to notice new ways to earn money. Maybe someone will ask you to pet sit for them, or a new position becomes available at work. Whatever you are given, be sure to take them even if they are things you haven't considered in the past.

Cast a Love and Attraction Spell

The Honey Jar Spell

This is part of most witches' spells 101, and it is a powerful and effective spell to boost relationships. This could be used for romantic purposes or to bring added strength to friendships. The honey spell is about creating intimacy and deeper connections, so casting it during the waxing moon phase will work even more effectively.

What You Need:

- Paper and pen
- A jar filled with honey
- A red candle for passionate love, a white candle for general purposes, or a pink candle for friendship

How to Cast the Spell

1. Write the name of the other person on the piece of paper.
2. Turn the paper around for 90 degrees and then write your name on the paper three times until it completely covers the other name on the paper.
3. Close your eyes and visualize what you see for the two of you in the future before you write that intention around the two names.
4. Now add the paper to the honey-filled jar – covering the paper completely.
5. Make sure you get some of the honey on your fingers before saying:

   "Just like this honey is sweet, that's how our relationship will be."

6. Slowly lick the honey from your fingers while you repeat the words of intent.
7. Seal the jar with a lid.
8. Place the appropriate candle on the top of the jar and light it.
9. Let the candle burn naturally, and let the wax seal the jar.
10. Store the jar away until the next waxing moon cycle.
11. Repeat the spell until you have achieved your desires.

Cast spells for joy, happiness, healing, social growth, pregnancy, and other attraction sources in the waxing moon, and your life will soon start to feel the benefit.

Magic for the Full Moon

There are three days when the power of the full moon is at its height. The day before and the day after the full moon are just as powerful as the actual day, and this is when you should perform your most impressive magic. In this part of the chapter, you will find simple ways to use the power of the full moon.

Charge Your Crystals

Create a space outside where you can see the full moon clearly. Ensure the space is clean and large enough for all your crystals to be without touching each other. Place a cloth on the space and carefully arrange your crystals so they benefit from the moonlight. Leave your crystals in the moonbeams for two hours and then take them back inside. They will be pure and clean and free from negative energy.

Release Things Holding You Back

This ritual helps you use the power of the archangels to help you move on. Invoke the archangel Haniel to aid you in this ritual before you perform it. Take a piece of paper and write down everything holding you back. Is it your job, or do you have bad habits? Are there things about your partner you wish were different, or do you need to detox your life?

When you have your list invoke the power of Haniel and thank him for his presence, light the paper on fire and close your eyes as you imagine your issues burning away into the atmosphere. When you open your eyes, watch the smoke leave and imagine it carrying your negativity with it. Close your eyes once more and ask Haniel if he has a message for you. Whatever flashes before you will give you the answer you need.

Full Moon Wish Spell

What You Need:

- A clear jar with a lid
- Rainwater that has been charged in the moonlight
- A silver coin
- A bell
- A silver candle

Choose a space where you can work in the moonlight and in full view of the moon. Hold the coin and focus on your desires, wishes, and what you want from life. Light the silver candle.

When you feel ready, drop the coin into the jar. Pour the water into the jar while you let it charge in the moonlight. When the water is smooth, and the reflection of the moon is clearly seen on the surface, say these words:

"This is my wish, and I ask that you grant it."

Ring the bell and then state your wish loudly and with intent. Repeat the process three times before placing the lid on the jar. Take the candle and drip some wax on the top of the lid before you thank the spirits for their help and go indoors with all your materials.

Keep the coin in the jar until you feel your wish has been granted or until the next full moon, when you can repeat the spell to reinforce your wishes.

Magic for the Waning Moon

Release and let go in this cleansing period of the moon. How does negativity affect you, and how can you become more positive? Magic and rituals performed in the waning moon period are especially effective when clearing out your spiritual and physical lives.

Cleansing Your Environment

Where do you feel the most protected and safe from negativity? Your home should be a haven, and your sacred space should all be clear from negativity, but just like regular cleaning, there are many different ways to cleanse your spaces. Some methods work better for some, while others are suitable for certain spaces where there are restrictive elements.

When to Cleanse Your Spaces

The rule of thumb is to cleanse whenever somewhere feels "off" or you don't feel as comfortable and safe as normal. However, sometimes you need to cleanse after certain events or before you perform certain rituals. Here are some of the most common:

- Your home after there have been disputes or arguments
- Your bed and bedroom after you have had nightmares or dreams that have left you anxious and stressed
- Your altar or sacred space after a spell has gone wrong or was ineffective

- There won't always be negative energy in your altar or sacred space after you have connected with spirits or ancestors. Still, it is important to clear residual energy between communications.
- Your tools and divination aids between readings and spells
- The bath or bathroom before you have a ritual bath
- Work areas after negative experiences and unsuccessful projects

Different Kinds of Cleansing Routines

Water Cleansing

The most available and adaptable way to cleanse is with pure water. Moon water is the most effective way to bring lunar energy to your space, but pure water also works. Fill a clear jug or bowl with water and ask the spirits to bless the liquid. Walk around your space clockwise, flicking the water around the perimeter. This method is effective for routine cleansing and is very budget-friendly.

Salt Clearing

This method is especially effective for hard surfaces and floors. Replace the water with sea salt and sprinkle it around the perimeter of your area. Leave it for an hour before you sweep it up and throw it away. Remember to remove the residue salt from the home and dispose of it away from your immediate environment. Be careful when cleansing a carpeted area, as the salt can sometimes react with the dye in carpets.

Musical Clearing

This method is a joyful way to get rid of dodgy vibes. You know the feeling when you aren't sure why, but the hairs on the back of your neck are standing up, and you just feel icky. Creepy vibes and nervous energy aren't ideal, so use this method for an injection of positivity and joy. Crank up your radio or get out an old-school record player and bust out music that speaks to you. Upbeat hip-hop or classic rock tunes work especially well and dispel that negativity and anxious energy. Choose music to suit your situation.

Smoke Cleansing

This traditional method uses herbs and smudge sticks to cleanse spaces. Of course, some spaces won't be suitable, and some people have issues with smoke. If the space is suitable, then use sage bundles and smudge sticks to fill the area with cleansing smoke to clear negativity and bad vibes.

Essential Oils Cleanse

This is a method used to clear spaces that have been subject to major disruptions. It is a heavy-duty cleanse that ensures the space is harmonized and negativity-free. Choose the oils you love or are suitable for the situation and anoint all four corners of the space with them. Use a diffuser to cover the rest of the area while you call on the spirits for their blessing.

Breath Cleansing

What if the space you need cleansing is within yourself, and you feel blocked? Clear your mind and aura with this simple routine and lift your spirits and mood. Clean your teeth and mouth thoroughly before you sit in a quiet place where you won't be disturbed. Breathe in for a count of 5 and breathe out for a count of 6. Visualize a calm and soothing place where you feel safe and imagine yourself in it. Feel a blanket of calm surround you as you repeat the breathing g exercise until you feel calm and settled.

Magic for the Dark Moon

When the moon has all but left the sky, this is the perfect time to honor your ancestors and explore your unconscious mind. Take a deep delve into your subconscious and do some serious soul-searching. Take a hot ritual bath with your favorite herbs and oils to release tensions and built-up trauma.

Use these methods to banish drama and get your life back on track:

Banishing Candle Method

What You Need:

- Two whole cloves of garlic
- Four whole peppercorns
- ¼ liter of olive oil
- Black candle
- Carving tool

Soak the garlic and peppercorns in olive oil for two days before the dark moon. Carve the word "drama" into the candle when it is time to perform the ritual. If you have more specific issues, use different words to represent what is troubling you. Anoint the candle with the oil using a downward motion. Let the oil run off until the candle is fully ready for use. Place it in a candle holder and light it beneath the dark moon at night. Say a few words to the spirits, let the candle completely burn away, and then bury the remnants.

Bury the Drama Method

Do you have long-standing issues that have followed you through history? Are you fed up with tiring issues that keep reappearing? Take a piece of paper and list the conflicts and issues troubling you. Be detailed and clear about the problem, and ensure you are happy with the list.

On the night of the dark moon, take a small hand shovel, some blessed dirt, and the paper containing your issues. Go somewhere far from your home and bury the paper deep in the ground. Place the blessed dirt on top of the site and leave. Walk away and don't look back.

Spell to Break a Bad Habit

The burying process is effective at the dark moon and can be used to eliminate a bad habit.

What You Need:

- Small wooden box
- Pen and paper
- Clove of garlic
- 2 pieces of rosemary
- Symbol of your bad habit (a cigarette lighter, for example)
- A handful of coins
- Spade

The first thing to remember is that habits are hard to quit, and you need to be sure it's what you want. Write all the reasons for quitting on paper and keep it somewhere you can see it whenever you want to remind yourself why you are on this path.

During the full moon, charge your wooden box in the moonlight before you place it in your sacred space for two weeks. Every time you think about your bad habit during those two weeks, place a coin in the box. At first, this will happen a lot, but it should become less regular as the weeks pass.

Add garlic and rosemary to the box on the first night of the dark moon. Place the symbol inside as well and close the lid. Take the time to mourn the loss of something that has been with you for a long time before you shut the lid completely, and maybe nail it down or glue it shut.

Bury the box somewhere you love. A place with running water is best, as the motion of the water will help to take away the intent. Walk away and don't look back.

Moon Magic Overview

Whatever the cycle or season, it is important to chart how you work with lunar energy. Take one night per quarter to sit beneath the moon and consider how you feel. Are you tired or energized by the energy? Do you feel any more connected at certain times, or is the moon an effective way to practice mindfulness for you? If you are a Wiccan practitioner, you will already know the power of the esbat, which is a pagan time of power.

Transition to a moon-centric life, benefit from its celestial power, and improve your crafting. Lunar witchcraft is overwhelming because it's so powerful, so start small and build up your expertise to enhance your regular life and crafting life.

Chapter 9: Spirit Guides

Ingesting psychoactive plants is believed to connect you to the plant elements of nature.⁴

Who is on your team? In your regular life, it could be your partner, your best friend, your family, someone at work who is always there for you, or someone from the gym who helps you work out. Your social circle is your team, filled with people you can trust, love, and have your back. But what about your spiritual team? Who is part of the team that guides you through your magical life, and how are they relevant in your regular life? This chapter is all about the spirit guides and how they are part of your life, even if you don't realize they are there.

In Western spiritualism beliefs, multiple types of guides are assigned to your team, and it is their spiritual purpose to act as a guide or protector to you. They may have been on your team in previous lives or may be new to this incarnation. Your team, just like your regular social circle, changes and adapts to your needs. Some guides will be with you from your first incarnation and will be there until you ascend, while others will pop in and out of your life when you need them.

Another fascinating fact about your spiritual team is that they may or may not have spent time on Earth as humans. Some may be from astral planes and extraterrestrial systems, while others may live in light planes. Some may be angels and archangels who are dedicated to guiding you no matter which religion you follow. It is a common misconception that angels and archangels only help Christians. In spiritual terms, they serve mankind and have no interest in your religious beliefs.

Your main spirit guide is always there for you and was assigned to your life – long before this earthly existence. They know every fiber of your being and will help you whenever needed. Spirit guides are benevolent and loving, and they never judge you or your actions but may intervene if they feel you are on the wrong path. They are dedicated to guiding you and helping you achieve a specific and dedicated purpose in your current lifetime. You have complete autonomy when making decisions; your spirit team will always help you get what you desire.

Are There Any Spirits to Avoid?

Of course, not all spirits are equal. The main thing to remember is that the energy you send into the world will mirror the energy of the spirits you attract. In regular life, you wouldn't just ask a stranger for advice; you need to know that the person is on the same moral plane as you are to get important information. Just like the advice you gave about connecting to deities, the spirits are the same. There are low-level vibrational beings who aren't matched to your frequency and should be avoided. They aren't necessarily malignant or harmful but can affect you if you connect to them.

You can just say goodbye and disconnect if you feel connected to a spirit that doesn't match your frequency. Don't be disrespectful; thank them as you would in regular communications and say a respectful goodbye. You need to use your intuition and common sense to determine who and what you connect to, so apply this to your spirit team and gather the most positive and effective spirits you can.

Meet the Team

1. Life Guides or Guardian Angels

These spirits are your go-to energies who never leave your side. They operate on a higher energy level than humans and are always ready to impart their knowledge and wisdom. You may already know who they are from your former lives. They may have a name and a recognizable form in your mind. They are the "office managers" of your team, and they know how to deal with chaos and will keep an eye on the rest of your team. They bring peace and love to your existence and are happy to be there. Remember to connect to your guardian angels by asking them about their background as a spirit. These conversations deepen your connection and help you understand their ethos.

2. Warriors and Protectors

These are your personal bodyguards who are dedicated to keeping you safe, both physically and spiritually. Have you ever had a gut feeling about something that made you rethink your actions or plans? That could be your warrior guide telling you that something isn't quite right.

Warrior spirits are incredibly enlightened and will work with you to filter out any adverse advice and guidance that isn't dedicated to helping you achieve your highest purpose. They will often appear to you as literal warriors, soldiers, or other defensive forms. If you happen to see a sumo wrestler or a Viking warrior in your dreams or visions, say hello to your warrior spirit guide.

3. Gatekeeper Guides

These are another protective form of the spirit. They act as your doorman and check everything that passes into your life. Gatekeepers are incredibly important, and they have access to your Akashic record. This is the spiritual blueprint of your life and contains information about your past, present and future lives. They only allow energy sources that are dedicated to bringing you high-level and loving forms of energy.

4. Teacher Guides

As the name indicates, these spirits are there to teach you lessons. They are incredibly wise and practical, and they will visit you when you are straying from the path you are on. They aren't judging you; they simply need to point out your choices and give you alternative ways to go. Some people fear their teacher guides but, in reality, they are some of the more effective guides you have. They appear to you when you need to assess your current situation and maybe change course.

5. Animal or Totem Guides

Modern witchcraft and pagans have "rediscovered" the power of the animal spirit. Some ancient cultures like the Chinese and American Indians have known for generations just how important spirit animals are, and you can benefit from your own connection to the animal world. Your spirit animals reflect your inner yearnings and personality. You will connect on many levels, and they will mirror your work ethic, your passions, and how you instinctively operate. Some people believe they can choose their spirit animal, but that isn't true. You may imagine you have connections with "cool "animals like dolphins or eagles, but your spirit animal chooses you. It could be a spider or a cat, a snake, or a dog. You need to meditate and reflect so your animal appears to you in your dreams or visions.

6. Ancestors

Many ancient cultures have rituals and ceremonies to celebrate the dead and their ancestors. They offer food and drink to the spirits of those who have passed over and welcome them back to earth. In modern witchcraft, you can also tap into the hidden energies of your relatives. They bring blood connections that are historical and personal. Meeting your ancestors and your family's spirits will help you feel part of your lineage and can be beautiful and life-changing. Some ancestral spirits will be members of your family you have known, while some of them will be long-dead relatives who lived way before your lifetime.

7. Trans-species

Modern life is very aware of trans and what it means in sexuality. Still, there are also trans spirits that embody the connection between mankind and the animal world. Consider ancient spirit guides and the forms they took to give you inspiration about what to expect. The Indian god Ganesha was a human form with an elephant's head. In contrast, Anubis, the Egyptian god, had the head of a jackal. Echidna in Greek mythology was half woman and half snake, while Ra, the Egyptian god, was a human man with a falcon's head.

Groups of Spirits that Fall into this Category

- **The Centaur** – From Greek mythology, this half-man/half-horse creature has gained more attention since the Harry Potter books and films. It originates from the times of the Minoan civilization. It is believed they were so impressed by other cultures who rode horses that they created the myth of the centaur.
- **The Harpy** – In both Greek and Roman tales, the harpy is a bird with a woman's head who was described as a "human vulture." They represent destructive winds and signify the clearance of negative energy.
- **The Gorgon** – The three sisters from Greek mythology who were the most terrifying therianthrope ever were the gorgons, who were women in every way except for their terrifying hair made of writhing and hissing serpents. Simply looking at them would render humans into half-man/half-horse stone, and it is believed they are the original representation of the fear of snakes. Some gorgons are depicted with scales and claws, but the most recognizable are the ones with reptilian hair.
- **The Mermaid** – The original legend came from Assyria and told of a beautiful maiden with the tail of a fish who had transformed herself into mermaid form in shame after she accidentally killed her human lover. These creatures often appear to help seamen and sailors and could be part of your spiritual team.

Other trans spirits include faeries, sphinxes, and fauns, and they can be playful and entertaining creatures who visit you when you need to experience truly magical energy.

8. Ascension and Soul Guides

Some of your guides will be directly related to your soul's age and the level of your ascension. If you are an old soul, you will be given a guide appropriate to your level. If you are new to the process, the same principle applies. Just as in regular life, you are given the information you need depending on your experience and soul age.

9. Plants

In shamanic practices, ingesting plants that have psychoactive elements is believed to connect you to the plant energies of nature. Shamans believe that plants are a major source of vibrant and living energy, and they hold rituals and ceremonies to celebrate this fact. Certain species of cacti and acacia can create the same experience, but they can be dangerous. Suppose you want to summon the spirits of the plant world. In that case, it is safer to concentrate on the symbolic plant world rather than the experiential experiences.

10. Ascended Master

These are the "celebrities" of the spirit world. They have lived as humans, and they have mastered the spiritual aspects of life. Their experience of spiritual transcending and their ability to rise above the cycle of reincarnation makes them the ultimate teachers - providing you with an insight into the divine. They are available to everyone who calls on them as long as their intentions are true and come from the right place. They aren't strictly part of your team but are always on the sidelines, ready to be called if needed. They have paid their karmic debt and mastered ascension.

Common Ascended Masters

- **Jesus** - The ultimate ascended master who gave his life to save mankind. He brings the energy of unconditional love and joy. He teaches and displays the ultimate form of forgiveness as he forgave those that crucified him.

- **The Archangels** - It seems dismissive to link all the Archangels in one group, but they are the epitome of what ascended masters look like. Each of the angels brings different qualities, and they can work together as a team within their ranks to help you. Study them and discover what they bring to your life before you call on these heavenly beings to become part of your team. Remember, the angels don't care if you are religious or not. They have bigger things to think about, and they have the ear of God.

- **Amoghasiddhi** - In Buddhism, this deity is the destroyer of envy and the bringer of accomplishment. He will help you overcome jealousy and get past your obstacles when needed.

- **Krishna** - The eighth incarnation of the Hindu god Vishnu Krishna is wise and compassionate, bringing healing and love to your life.
- **Milarepa** - The famous Tibetan yogi who founded the school of Tibetan Buddhism and is a spiritual embodiment of joy. He is famous for his poetry and songs and will inspire you to be more creative and loving.
- **Mother Teresa** - The Albanian Catholic nun who taught the world the meaning of true compassion and was a leading light in the Church. Call on her for kindness and love when you feel like you need more humanity in your life.

How to Connect to Your Spirit Guides

You can use the same methods as described in the chapter about gods and goddesses, and you will get a response. The methods below are more dedicated to certain groups and spirits and intensify your intent which is the base of all good magic.

Ancestors

Your ancestors are waiting for you in the spirit world, and there are many ways to connect to them. Start a family tree and research your ancestors. So many online resources are available that it is easy to find where you came from. Another way to connect to your more recent ancestors is to use objects that once belonged to them. Maybe you have a piece of jewelry or a favorite item of clothing that you associate with your relatives. Hold it close and let your mind clear of anything except your memories. Ask them to visit you, share their life experiences, and guide you for the future.

Your ancestors will respond and bring the unmistakable feeling of family to your life. You will feel uplifted and joyful. Increase this connection by wearing your items or displaying them in your home. There doesn't have to be a shrine to your relatives, just a place where you can remember them and be thankful for their influence.

The Archangels or Other Ascended Masters

Connecting to the highest members of the spiritual realm is daunting for beginners, but that doesn't mean you shouldn't try. The spirits have a hierarchy, but they are also benevolent beings dedicated to helping humankind live better lives. They won't ever push themselves forward or interfere if you don't ask first. They respect free will and your personal choices and will never visit unless summoned.

Research your spirits and get to know them just like you did with the gods and goddesses. What did they achieve on Earth? What were they known for, and why are you drawn to them? Your instinct will tell you whom to communicate with and why.

Simple Steps to Better Communication

Step 1 - Get into the Habit of Asking

When you encounter smaller problems during your regular life, try calling on spirits or the universe for help. The more you ask, the more you will receive, and the process will become more natural. Think of them as a helpline that is always there and ready to take your call.

Step 2 - Make a List of What You Need

Vague doesn't work with spirit guides. The clearer your requests are (and the more details you provide), the more effective your spirit guides are. Take the time to list the top issues in your life and what effect they are having on your life. Be concise yet clear, and write them down with intent and belief that this is the first step in dealing with your issues.

Step 3 - Listen and See the Signs

Once you have put your requests out there, the onus is on you to recognize the signs you are sent.

Signs Your Spirits Are Communicating with You

- **You feel peaceful and calm.** If you feel as if someone is looking over your shoulder and keeping you safe, it helps you feel comforted. Fear and doubt leave you, and you feel optimistic and joyful.

- **You see signs that mean something to you.** The spirits are playful and like to mix it up a bit when it comes to communicating. They will send signs and symbols that are personal to your life and repeat them until you have dealt with your issues. Watch out for repeated symbols that have special meanings to you.

- **You get sudden ideas and insights** - If you get a "lightbulb moment" after you have asked for help from the spirit world, it could be a communication from them. They have the power to send you mental images or ideas to guide you in the right direction.
- **You receive information from unexpected sources.** If you suddenly see an opportunity to do something that wasn't there before, it could indicate the presence of spiritual aid. They will give you chances to take specific actions that might not make sense but will help you if you are brave enough to take them. Trust your instincts and the fact that this information will help you.
- **Physical sensations.** Some people say they feel physical sensations when they connect to the spirits. Warm-tingling feelings and pressure in certain areas could indicate they are with you.
- **Physical signs.** Spirits are great at sending you signs from nature that show they are around. Feathers are a popular choice and often appear to show you aren't alone. Some say birds appear in their garden when they lose a loved one or another random animal suddenly appears. Watch out for these signs and say thank you when you see them.

Ground Yourself after Connecting to the Spirit World

Connecting to the spirits is a physical and mental process. Eventually, you will have to return to your physical form on Earth. The energy shift you experience isn't practical for regular life, so you need to ground yourself and become involved in the wholly human existence your body is used to. Here are some simple methods to return to the planet and regain your equilibrium:

- Stamp your feet and feel the energy drain into the ground below your feet.
- Sit on a stone or rock and let the energy be absorbed by its natural material.

- Take care of yourself with a drink or snack to show you are back in charge of looking after yourself.
- Create a barrier by imagining a white light surrounding you. Once you are in your bubble, you will return to your natural state.

Remember that all the suggestions in this chapter won't work for everyone, but they do give you a blueprint for your communications. The spirits are there for you and will help you become part of the spiritual universe.

Chapter 10: Ritual Magic

Ritual magic may sound like something that is only available for advanced witches and practitioners. It sounds like the epic form of magic that needs to be studied and practiced for effective results. It does involve art and science, and it helps you to transform and change your life so that you become empowered and can create the life you choose. It is a magic practice that allows you to harness the abilities of your racial memory and tap into the powers and memories of humanity through time.

When the ancient Egyptians practiced ritual magic, their knowledge and practices became part of that collective story of magic. When Babylonians or Hindu cultures created new ways to communicate with the spirits and demons of their beliefs, that knowledge was also added to the primordial magic soup waiting for you to dine upon.

Your unconscious mind will be reminded of these racial memories and knowledge without you realizing it, and it will allow you to recognize symbols and signs from history. The collective realms of magic, higher thoughts, dreams, and creation are there for you and have been around since the dawn of creation. Across the world, different cultures have been practicing ritual magic, and they didn't limit their beliefs to science. Only in the last few generations have humans regressed into the childish belief that if they can't recognize something with their physical senses, then it isn't and can't be true. Humans have become a race of people who think if they can't measure it, then it doesn't exist.

Ritual Magic in Today's Terms

Ritual magic is one of the most powerful forms of magic, and it can give you direct access to higher energies from countless realms that will bring real changes to your life. It is performed with all parts of yourself and immerses your mind, soul, body, and deepest intentions in the ritual so the ceremony and the magic become like another extension of yourself. The practice, also known as ceremonial magic, gained popularity in the late 19th and early 20th centuries.

An influx of pagan beliefs and occult practices meant that ceremonies and rituals became more popular, and the occultist Alastair Crowley was one of the most effective advocates. The ceremonies and rituals were steeped in secrecy to ensure the practitioners were able to perform their ceremonies without recrimination. Today, the practice is more open and involves deepening your focus and building your practice, so the magic is more powerful. It isn't a practice for casual magic. This will change your life and how you engage with your subconscious mind. It is a step further on your journey and will help you embrace a life of transformation and progression.

Ritual Magic Techniques

Previous chapters have covered some more popular techniques like divination, invoking, and evoking spirits and deities. Other techniques happen in ceremonial magic, like the Eucharist magic ritual that has evolved from Christianity and involves the digestion of regular foods that have been made divine. This is called Holy Communion, an important part of the Christian belief.

Consecration is another form of ceremonial magic involving dedicating a space or person as a sacred sphere used for a magical purpose and service.

Banishing is the most used form of ritual magic and can be used to remove non-physical influences from your life. One of the more effective rituals is the Lesser Banishing Ritual of the Pentagram, described below.

The Lesser Banishing Ritual of the Pentagram

This ritual magic will give a greater insight into how the process works and the power of your intent. It can be adapted to your needs and requirements and the deities and spirits with whom you work.

Step 1. Stand in the middle of a sacred space and face east. Imagine you are a giant sculpture looking down on the planet as a tiny sphere in your eye line. You are the center of the universe, and everything revolves around you. Look up and see the bright white light that emanates from above you and pull it down to your forehead.

Step 2. Hold the beam of light as if it was a dagger, and repeat the word ATAH as you feel the vibrations.

Step 3. Move your right hand down your body, passing over your throat, chest, and groin area as you feel the white light running right through you. There is now a beam of white energy and light running from the top of the universe to the Earth, and it passes right through your body. Say the word MALKUTH as you feel the connection form.

Step 4. Raise your hand to your right shoulder and imagine the white light is drawn to that point. Now visualize the light emanating from your shoulder and into the universe. Say the word VEGEBOORA as the light passes through you.

Step 5. Repeat the process with your left shoulder, replacing the word with VEGEDOOLA.

Step 6. Now center yourself by raising your arms to your chest as if you were praying and clasp them together. Say the words LAYOLAM AMEN. You are now the central part of a cross with light emanating from you to the very edges of the universe. You are now the ruler of your universe and the creator of your destiny.

Step 7. Now face the east and trace a large five-sided pentagram with your finger. Imagine that lines are formed by flaming, bright-blue lights, and the pentacle glows with the power of a thousand lamps. Bring your hands back to the side of your head and point your fingers forward. As you do so, thrust your left foot before you and say the word YODAYVAVHEH. This is the Hebrew signal of the enterer and shows the universe your intent to march forward and to capture the energy of your life.

Feel the divine energy running through you and being absorbed by the pentagram. Take your left foot and replace it in its former position so you are standing straight. Now raise your left hand and put your index finger to your mouth to signal silence. Your right arm should remain extended and pointing to the pentagram.

Step 8. Start to walk backward to the southern part of your area with your finger still retaining a connection to the blue pentagram. Create a white line of blazing energy between yourself and the symbol. As you reach the southernmost point, you will have created a circle of energy between the symbol and yourself.

Trace another pentagram in the air and say the word ADONAY as you see the flames burst into life. Repeat this process in the west as you vibrate the word EEHAYYAY. Do the same in the north, saying AGALA, and then walk to the east to complete the circle.

Step 9. Look at the circle you have created. Four magnificent pentagrams at the cardinal points of your space, all joined by a circle of pure white energy.

Step 10. Step into the center of the area, recreate the magical cross of Kabbalistic energy and invoke the angel Gabriel by saying his name. Imagine he is standing behind you dressed in magnificent robes of orange and blue, and his favored element, water, is flowing onto your back.

Step 11. Now open your eyes and look to the right of yourself and say, "On my right, Michael," and visualize the archangel of fire standing beside you. His robes are red and green, and you can feel the heat of his favorite element, fire, heating your body.

Step 12. Extend your arms and invoke the archangel of air, RAPHAEL and visualize him standing in his robes of yellow and violet and feel the cooling energy of his element, air, on your face and body.

Step 13. Look over your left shoulder and invoke the archangel of earth, AURIEL, dressed in russet and green robes. Feel the solidity of his energy enter your body and make you feel grounded and safe.

Step 14. Take a minute to visualize what you have created. An amazing circle of energy with a blazing pentagram and the presence of archangels. Say,

"*Around me shines these pentagrams,*"

and now trace the shape of a hexagon in a brilliant orange fire on your breast. Say,

"*Within me shines the power of the six-pointed star.*"

as you finish the ritual.

Use this ritual to banish negativity and ask the archangels to change your life and imbue you with the strength of the universe. This circle is impenetrable and will protect you from all negative forces and influences.

How to Cast a Wiccan Ritual Magic Circle

This is a simple protection ritual that you can perform anywhere and can be modified to suit your needs and the time of year you are performing your magic. Use the wheel of the year to help you choose ritualistic items that celebrate the power of nature. If you are short on space, just use the four-candle part of the ritual for a temporary and effective ritual.

1. Choose a space and set the scene by playing music that inspires you as you work.
2. Cleanse the area with a ritual broom only used for magic, not regular housework, helping you set the scene.
3. Use candles to mark the cardinal points of the room. Red for the south, blue for the west, green for the north, and yellow for the east.
4. Move clockwise and light the candles while saying a prayer of thanks to your chosen spirits or deities.
5. Use markers to form a circle between the candles. Natural objects like branches or flowers work and increase the connection to nature.
6. Take a bowl of water and bless it with these words:

   "I consecrate this liquid to make it fit for a place in my sacred circle, and I ask that it is blessed by the Mother and Father Gods (or your chosen deities) and are capable of repelling evil."
7. Now take a bowl of salt and say these words:

   "I ask the Mother and Father to consecrate this salt and make it fit to dwell within the sacred circle."
8. Imagine the water and salt dispersing all the negative energy in the room and leaving behind a cleansed and sacred space. Walk around the circle and say the following words:

   "Here is my sacred boundary; let nothing but love enter,

   There will be no negativity in this space,

   It is sacred and free from evil,

   So let it be."
9. Sprinkle the salt around the circle and seal it against negative energy. Say your favored chants and ask your preferred spirits to join you.

Your circle is now cast. This is your ritual magic space, and it can be used to call on the universe to make your life more effective and successful.

Tips for Ritual Magic

There are many rituals you can perform within your sacred space, and you should choose ones that suit your needs. The main things to remember about ritual or ceremonial magic are:

1. Stay safe. Create a sacred space that is strong and pure and will keep out negative energies and spirits that may not be fully on your wavelength.
2. Use tools to help your magic intentions become more pronounced. See the list below for a quick start-up guide for magic tools.
3. Use astrology to strengthen your spells and rituals. We have already covered lunar magic, but you can also use your zodiac sign to help you work when it is more effective. The stars will help you find your most powerful times of the year and when to perform certain spells.
4. Use your divination tools like tarot and the runes as part of your ritual magic. They may show you alternative ways to craft your spells.
5. Consider the ethics and morality of your magic. Are you true to your basic principles? Never perform magic that goes against your morals and beliefs, even when it seems advantageous to do so. Your intentions should always be true and free from negative emotional influences.

Magic Tools and How to Use Them

- **The Athame** – A magic dagger that represents the element of air and the sharpness of the mind. Use it to cast your circles and direct energy in your spells and rituals.

- **A Cup** – A ritual cup should only be used for magic purposes. Never use it to drink a cup of coffee or other regular liquids. The cup represents the element of water and is used to share libations or offer them to the deities and spirits. It represents the breath of your unconscious and the emotional ties to magic.

- **A Wand** – Traditionally made from wood or metal, a wand is an extension of the user and represents the will of the person wielding it. Use it to direct energy and increase focus.
- **Lamp** – Some practitioners prefer to use a lamp for spells rather than candles or fire, as they are a hazard. A lamp represents the element of spirit and the godhood within us all. It is also used to bring the power of the Holy Guardian Angel to your work.
- **The Besom** – This is a broom usually made from natural materials that are bound by willow strands. You can buy them from shops, but the most effective besoms are handmade. Use your favorite wood and create a besom for sweeping and clearing your sacred space.
- **The Pentacle** – Not to be confused with the pentagram, which is the five-sided figure used in the Lesser Banishing Ritual of the Pentagram. A pentacle is a flat piece of wood, metal, clay, or wax that is decorated with magical symbols. Once again, you can buy highly decorative pentacles from magical stores and online resources, but the most effective are ones that you create yourself. The pentacle is used as a base for your other magical tools and brings extra meaning to your work.
- **Robes** – The clothes you wear can make a huge difference in your crafting. Just like in regular life, preparing for your rituals and spellcasting should be thorough and done with intent. If you are going to your regular work, you dress appropriately in clothing that is suitable and fit for purpose. The same principle works for magic. Dress in loose and comfortable robes but make the occasion special with certain colors or styles of the robe. Your clothing helps you to get into the perfect state of mind for your work and focuses your attention.

Bonus Chapter: The Herbal Glossary

Witchcraft is all about using natural products to create magical potions and spells, but knowing what each ingredient brings to the situation is important. This list gives you basic knowledge which you can add to and helps you create an herb glossary that will help you with any spells you try.

Allspice - Brings money, prosperity, and luck to your magic. Also helps digestion and can be used as a general anesthetic.

Basil - Success in business opportunities and money. Brings calm energy and peaceful vibes to your crafting. When added to your cooking, it can also cure flatulence.

Bay Leaves - Used in banishment spells and exorcisms, bring fidelity and love to spells for relationships and strengthens wish magic. Use for stronger energies in spells to create luck, love, and passion.

Cayenne - Speeds up spells and brings extra strength to magic. Overcomes grief and loss and helps to aid separation.

Cloves - Stops gossip and aids protection.

Dill Weed - Luck, money, prosperity, and protection.

Fennel - Increased mental strength, helps weight-loss spells and brings fortitude and strength.

Garlic - Makes other ingredients more effective, protects against psychic vampires, and repels evil.

Ginger - Healing, soothing energy and creates new opportunities, and strengthens resolve.

Marjoram - Increased energy in ancestral magic, animal connections, and helps lucid dreaming, and is soothing.

Mandrake - Legendary magical herb for love magic, passion, relationship issues, protection, and curses

Marjoram - Protection. Helps marriages find common ground, calms the mind, eases grief, and aids in coming to terms with death.

Marshmallow Root - Love charms and amulets, increases psychic powers, protection, attracting positive spirits.

Meadowsweet - The sacred flower of spring, helps any new ventures and helps emotional rebirth.

Mistletoe - Good luck, love, and money spells, attracting potential life partners.

Mugwort - Mirror and water scrying, divination, psychic ability, astral travel, improves the chance of lucid dreaming, Lunar magic.

Mullein - Protection, illumination, clear mental health, bravery and courage, hedge-crossing, Crone magic.

Nettle - Courage, making spells more sacred, protection, healing, warding off evil.

Nutmeg - Brings luck, prosperity, and financial success.

Onion Flowers - Burn to banish bad habits and negative influences. Use raw onions to protect your home and keep evil spirits away.

Orange Peel - Raises vibrations and centering solar herb of joy, blessings, love, and good luck.

Orris Root - Love amulets and charms, increases powers of persuasion, increases popularity, charisma, and success.

Patchouli - Love and sex magic, attraction, fertility, rites of passage, and leaving adolescence behind.

Pennyroyal - Peace, increases mental and physical strength, patience, removing anger, warding.

Peppermint - Mental healing, overall purification, psychic awareness, love, and passion.

Pine - Persistence. Increases modesty, prosperity, financial health, and good health.

Quince - Good luck, happiness, protection. Carry quince seeds in a red bag to keep yourself safe from attack.

Raspberry Leaf - Love and romance, temptation, divination.

Red Sandalwood - Used in incense for meditation, healing, and inducing trance work.

Rose - Used in charms of love and beauty, harmony, and divination; it increases self-confidence.

Rosemary - Cleansing, purification and spirituality, vitality and energy, wisdom and knowledge, protection.

Rowan - Protection, enhanced psychic connections.

Rue - Protection, exorcism, purifying, passion charms, and protective charms.

Solomon's Seal Root - All-round protection against evil and negative energy.

Spearmint - Love and passion, psychic strength, cleansing, rebirth, protecting property and belongings.

Star Anise - Divination, good fortune, psychic dreams, travel charms, astral traveling.

Thyme - Inner beauty, strength, courage, a favorite herb of spirits.

Valerian - Protection, removing enemy spells, dispelling negativity, Egyptian magic.

Vervain - Old World herb of wisdom, knowledge, healing, and prophecy.

White Sage - Cleansing, house protection, trance work, healing, and mental clarity.

White Willow Bark - Peace, wisdom, knowledge, attracting love that will last, divination, lunar magic.

Wild Lettuce - Inducing visions, trance, dream magic, astral travel, and improved sleep patterns.

Witch Hazel - Comfort and healing, wisdom, protection, comfort, and dealing with grief, dispels anger and negativity.

Woodruff - Success and achievements. Put woodruff in your left shoe, and your team will win.

Wormwood - Induces psychic vision, connections to the spirit world, strengthens hexes and curses, and removes any negative spells that have been cast against you.

Yarrow - Ancient medicinal flower used for courage, divination, and good fortune.

Conclusion

What a wild ride that was! Hopefully, you are all set for your new magical journey and are looking forward to your future. You have the knowledge, the expertise, and the intent, so all you need now is that first step. Become part of this brave new world filled with positivity and love. Be safe and happy with your crafting, and you will soon be ready to share your new passions with other members of the magical community. There are so many reasons to become involved, so don't wait another minute. Good luck, not that you need it, and enjoy your experiences.

Part 2: Smudging

The Ultimate Guide to Spiritual Cleansing, Psychic Protection, and Energy Clearing

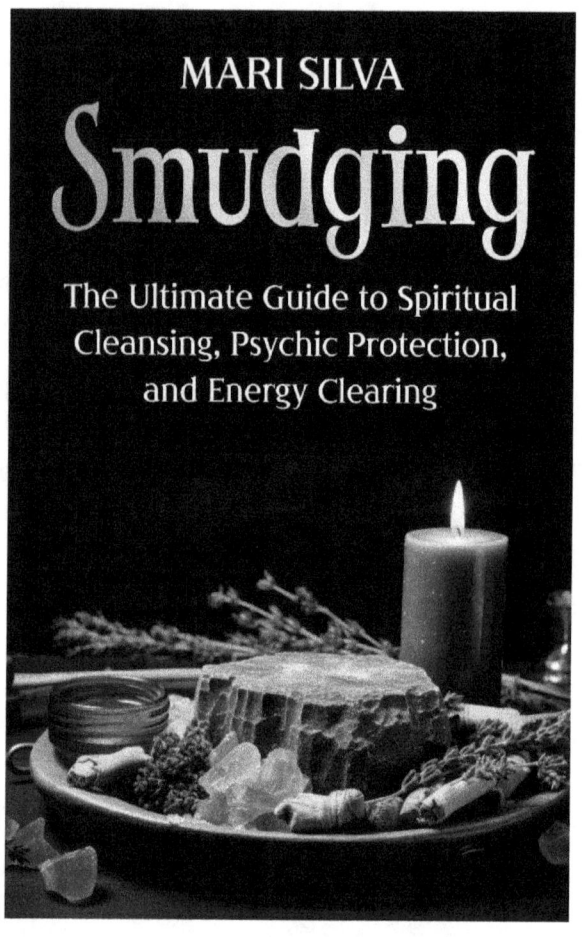

Introduction

When someone mentions "smudging your home," what thoughts come to mind? Do you feel a bit intimidated? Maybe it sounds complicated, messy, or weird. Even though smudging has gained popularity in recent years, many people still feel overwhelmed by the idea of smudging their homes. It's understandable to be skeptical or unsure, thinking it may involve a lot of smoke and strange religious rituals. Some may even find the whole process too complex. Sometimes, even with the intention and enthusiasm to smudge, people give up at the first hurdle — finding a smudge stick to buy!

Like anything new, it's helpful to understand the benefits of the process you're considering. Why should you smudge your home? Is it actually necessary? Can you make it simple and enjoyable? Are there alternative ways to clear the energy in your home? And what makes smudging so special? Think of a ritual like dating, for example. The more questions you ask, the sooner you'll know if it's worth investing in this relationship. The word "relationship" is used in the sense that entering the world of smudging ideally means entering a beautiful, long-term connection. Like any relationship, you'll have to go through many stages to reach a place of deep intimacy and commitment.

In this book, you'll get the answer to all of your questions and learn various ways to smudge, including some very simple techniques you can enjoy more than once a day. The energy in your home can shift after a long day, bringing along busy, hectic, and sometimes negative energies from outside. In such situations, a quick two-to-three-minute smudging session can work wonders to calm and purify the space and cleanse your energy. The beauty of smudging is that it can be as simple and quick or as elaborate and intricate as you want. Once you grasp the basics and explore optional add-ons, you'll feel more empowered to create your own rituals which suit your situation.

Smudging can be an easy, centering, enjoyable, and grounding experience. However, you'll notice, above all else, the ability to purify energy in your space. By the time you have finished reading this book, you'll feel confident, empowered, and ready to take charge of the energy in your home—and your life—through smudging. You'll be excited and enthusiastic about creating a whole new level of positive energy in your own space.

Chapter 1: The Power of Smudging

Smudging is an ancient form of cleansing used on a person, an object, or a space using the smoke of burning herbs. The herbs can be any of the following; dried sage, sweetgrass, lavender, cedar, rosemary, and other plants with beneficial properties. Smudging (or smoke cleansing) purifies the energy of the object or person in focus. Since ancient times, different cultures have had their own unique traditions for smudging. These traditions often involved prayers, meditations, or other rituals. For example, in some Native American cultures, sweetgrass is burned during an elaborate ceremony meant to release the positive energy

Smudging purifies the energy of the object or person in focus."

of the sacred plant into the air. Whatever your reason for wanting to spiritually cleanse an area, object, or person, this chapter will introduce you to the practice of smudging, explore its background, explain how it works, and explore its benefits.

How Does Smudging Work?

The practice of smudging is relatively simple; it only has a few fundamental tenets:

- Smudging relies on setting an intention. For example, you form an intention to cleanse your space of negative energy or invite positive energy into your home.
- Once your intention is set, light the herb and allow it to become engulfed in flames until it begins to smoke. Always do this, bearing in mind safety factors. Then, waft the smoke around a person's body, a space, or an object with your hand or using a feather. If purifying the body, start at the feet and move up to the head.
- When purging a space or an object, windows must be open, or you can perform the ritual outdoors.
- During cleansing, imagine the manifestation of your intention – you see the negative energy leaving you and positive vibes surrounding you, the object, or the space in question.
- Once you have cleansed yourself, the object, or your space, you should extinguish the herb safely and thank it for its service.
- Some practitioners love to finish their smudging ritual with a closing prayer or mantra. You can recite this when you feel negativity around yourself, the person or object you wanted to purify has left, or when you've finished cleansing a space.
- Whether you perform the closing part or not, it's recommended that you repeat your intention before closing the ceremony.
- The absence of negativity and positive changes in the person, object, or environment are indicators of smudging's effectiveness.
- The frequency of smudging depends on the practice – it can be done annually, during festivities, or as frequently as you feel the need to ward off negativity.

Smudging in Different Cultures

Smudging -or burning herbs to purify the energy of a space - has enjoyed a resurgence of popularity in recent years as more and more people are exploring alternative lifestyles. Its origins are in ancient civilizations and have long been associated with Native American and Indigenous cultures. In Native American cultures, the smudging ritual involves using a bundle of sage, sweetgrass, cedar, tobacco, or other herbs that have been dried and bound together into a slow-burning purification tool. Sometimes entire leaves or branches are placed in a fireproof container and lit until they begin smoking, and the smoke is then used to cleanse the area or person of negative energy. A person who smoke-cleanses one or more people can lead the ritual instead of depending on a regular practitioner. They either blow the smoke out toward the recipient or space, or the recipient inhales the smoke. According to Native American beliefs, inhaled herbal smoke heals a person's entire being. When the plants burn down, their ashes are returned to their origin - usually by scattering them on the bare ground. It is believed that ashes absorb negative energy, so discarding them helps you to dispose of that negativity. Smudging is also used during prayer or meditation and for connecting with the spirit world.

Native Americans have different beliefs regarding the benefits of each herb used for smudging. For example, they praise sweetgrass for drawing in positive vibes and cedar for facilitating blessings and cleansing the body from disease. Sage, which they believe can ward off any form of negativity, has a unique origin story. According to a Native American legend, the herb sage first appeared a very long time ago when a village was full of negativity. Everyone felt bad about themselves and others, and everything seemed to be going wrong for everyone. One day, a young man showed up carrying a bundle of herbs in his arms. He introduced the herb to the villagers as sage, a plant that can empower anyone to handle negativity. He built a fire, lit the sage, and showed the villagers how to smudge themselves. The villagers started to feel good about themselves and began to experience success in their endeavors. The young man disappeared, but the villagers noticed that sage had begun to grow in their area. So, they started using it regularly for cleansing.

For centuries, Shamans have believed that smudging is a powerful way to clear negative energy and create a sense of balance and harmony in any space. As the smoke travels through the air, it is believed to have the power to cleanse a space of negative energies while creating positive feelings and raising vibrations. In shamanic traditions, smudging involves a prayer or ritual, after which the smoke is sent into the four cardinal directions. Besides this, different practitioners and tribes have diversified methods and techniques for smudging, including when and how it's used. Shamans readily use smudging for divination and cleansing when preparing for a rite or ceremony. Modern practitioners also use it to restore emotional, physical, and mental balance, ward off negativity, and enhance their shamanic practices. They also smudge their magical tools and sacred spaces - often before and after use - to restore balance. Some even smoke-cleanse themselves daily to maintain a centered state of being, which enables them to reach a trance-like state for their meditative practices.

Native Americans and Shamans also recommended smudging when someone had been in contact with a sick person (physically or mentally), emotionally unbalanced individuals, or those who had been otherwise affected by negative influences.

Benefits of Smudging

As you'll see in the text below, smudging has numerous benefits for your physical, mental, spiritual, and emotional well-being.

Spiritual

One of the fundamental benefits of smudging is its spiritual aspect. This stems from the belief that when practiced in sacred ceremonies, smoke cleansing sends away any built-up negative energy and attracts positive intentions from nature, allowing you to manifest your desires more easily. It isn't used to obtain spiritual awareness and connection to one's higher self in many Native and Indigenous cultures for no reason! Moreover, by focusing on each individual herb during your ritual, you will be able to connect with its medicinal properties and obtain powerful healing agents for physical, emotional, and mental health issues. Once you reach the healing stage, you'll be even more empowered to ward off stress-inducing negative vibes.

Smudging can help you heal from negative influences from past traumas, malicious people in your environment, or bad experiences in any aspect of your life. Your sense of smell is linked to instinct and memory recall functions, which is another reason the aroma of smudged herbs can help you work through stress and traumatic events. As you inhale their soothing scent, the herbs will help you allay the fear, anger, anxiety, grief, and triggers you associate with past traumas.

Restoring your energetic balance after these events fosters a positive attitude for meditation and spiritual rituals. Not only that, but certain herbs contain bioactive compounds that, when inhaled, improve intention-setting abilities and insight. Whether you use it for spiritual practices or self-improvement, clearing out negativity from and around you will benefit your spiritual well-being.

Certain herbs are blessed with protective abilities. Smudging them can help you ward off evil forces and psychic attacks during spiritual work. They help chase away negative thoughts triggered by outside influences and create a shield around you to repel similar intrusions in the future. The protective effects of smudging can also come in handy when dealing with difficult people or preparing to handle particularly challenging situations.

Smudging enhances creativity in all aspects of life. Whatever problem you're trying to solve, purifying yourself with cleansing smoke will help you find innovative solutions. It can boost your productivity by inspiring you with new ideas. If you're an artist experiencing a creative block, the herbs can reveal new pathways for your creative juices to flow.

The cleansing and purifying properties of herbs burned while smudging can open up intuition, encouraging you to start trusting your gut feelings. If you feel like your judgment is clouded and this is blocking your intuition, practicing smudging could enable your inner psychic senses to reveal themselves. By becoming familiar with your psychic gifts, you sharpen your intuition and keep it clear of judgmental or biased ideas and beliefs.

Lastly, smudging is good for spiritual practices because it encourages self-love. After all, there is no better way to begin exploring and working on your spirituality than by accepting yourself. Some believe this benefit comes from the burned herbs' ability to open and unblock chakras associated with self-love and acceptance.

Psychological

One of the most outstanding benefits of smoke cleansing is its ability to help reduce stress and anxiety levels. This can be achieved through the calming effects of the herbs' aromas. Burning herbs like sage or cedar releases a pleasant aroma that promotes calmness and relaxation in the body and mind.

Certain herbs contain phytochemicals that stimulate anti-excitatory receptors and neurotransmitters in the brain, effectively relieving anxiety symptoms. Because of their ability to chase away harmful feelings, smudging can uplift your mood quickly. Regularly cleansing with sage could help you manage your symptoms if you suffer from depression or other mood-related conditions.

Energetic

Smudging promotes a sense of clarity, boosts the sensation of calmness and peace, improves your energy levels, and fosters self-awareness. This smudging benefit stems from the herbs' ability to encourage mindful presence during rituals. The energetic influence of the herbs used in smudging enables you to actively engage with all five senses. By empowering you energetically, certain burned herbs can also foster clear thinking and quick reactions, making it easier for you to pick up spiritual signals through your senses. If boosting your mood doesn't make you consider trying your hand at smudging, the possibility of improved clarity and awareness certainly will.

When you feel more energized, your mind is sharp, enabling you to think more positively and develop helpful and productive thought patterns. This proves that positive energy has a higher vibrational frequency. Besides making you feel good physically, emotionally, and mentally, smudging will also improve your cognitive function. This could help you combat the effects of neurodegenerative conditions like Alzheimer's disease and dementia. The reason for this lies in the effect of smoked herbs on your hormones. Many mental and neurodegenerative conditions develop due to adrenal fatigue – a state caused by hormonal misbalance of the adrenal glands, which occurs during stress. In a similar vein, healthy people's loss of neurons can also result in stress-induced fatigue. As a result, you may suffer from cognitive impairments, even if you don't have a neurodegenerative or mental health condition. This often happens due to inflammatory conditions in the body, which inevitably affect the nervous system. Whether accompanied by anxiety, impaired cognitive functions, or any other symptoms, conditions affecting cognitive and mental health can make the sufferer feel that relief is impossible to achieve. The energizing effect of smudging can chase away these negative thoughts, empowering the person to find efficient solutions and, more importantly, relief for their symptoms. The two most important hormones released by the adrenal glands, norepinephrine and epinephrine, must be in balance to achieve this. Cortisol, serotonin, and dopamine – more hormones responsible for controlling energy levels – are also positively affected by smudging. The smoke of certain herbs restores the optimal timing for the release of these chemicals.

Certain herbs have a proven beneficial effect on your chakra system – the complex entity representing your energy. The chakra system has seven main access points, known as chakras. The chakras are responsible for the healthy flow of energy through your body. If any of them is blocked or not working properly, this affects your entire energy system. Smudging herbs associated with the individual chakras (or all of your chakras) can help clear them out. As you unblock your energy centers, you cleanse, shield, and re-energize your mind, body, and soul. For example, rosemary can open up your heart chakra, enabling you to develop (self) compassion and understanding. Likewise, the same herb can unblock your third eye chakra, the energy center responsible for spiritual clarity and psychic awareness.

Physical

Another way smudging can boost your energy is by improving the quality of your sleep. Negative energy influences often leave you with sleepless nights. Or, even if you manage to sleep for a few hours, you feel more tired after waking up than before going to bed. Smudging before sleep can ward off any negative energies hindering your sleep, allowing you to feel energized and productive throughout the following day. It will help you fall asleep faster and grant you uninterrupted sleep – and if you do wake up during the night, you'll fall back asleep instead of being plagued by worries about the coming day.

Beyond normalizing your sleep patterns, smoke from smudging can also help improve your skin and boost the function of many organs and organ systems, including the respiratory, gastrointestinal, and circulatory systems. The air-purifying effects of the smoke mean that your skin will be exposed to fewer pollutants, allowing it to heal and regenerate. Due to its sleep-and energy-boosting benefits, smudging will make your skin look positively radiant and rejuvenated. Likewise, pure air will improve your lung function and combat the symptoms of chronic and acute respiratory conditions.

Certain herbs have analgesic properties, meaning they can bring relief to headaches, heartburn, muscle aches, and joint pains. The anti-inflammatory compounds in herbs like sage, rosemary, and others further emphasize this benefit.

Some herbs can also boost immune function, helping you to ward off infections and combat existing ones. They foster immune cell production and improve the function of all body parts responsible for healthy immunity, including the bone marrow, spleen, thymus, gut, and skin.

Moreover, the soothing effects of smudged herbs can lower your heart rate and blood pressure, positively contributing to your heart health. When feeling anxious or stressed, inhaling herbal smoke regulates your breathing pattern, allowing you to take more oxygen into your body. This further enhances the healing effects of smudging, as oxygen is needed for neutralizing free radicals – the byproducts of oxidative stress and the precursors of many physical and mental health conditions.

Environmental

Smoke cleansing has also been proven to have antiseptic properties. In other words, the smoke from the herbs can effectively purify the air in any room containing viruses, fungi, or bacteria that can cause common respiratory issues or illnesses like asthma, colds, and flu. Besides the aforementioned microorganisms and their byproducts, herbs used in smudging can eliminate potential allergens like dust, pollen, mold spores, and pet dander – relieving those insufferable allergy symptoms. This is why smoke cleansing is ideal for disinfecting indoor spaces without using harmful chemicals or sprays.

Cleaner air is known for improved oxygen concentration levels, making the atmosphere perfect for studying or working on assignments requiring intense focus and a wider attention span. Certain herbs, like sage, are also known for their insect-repellent abilities. Let's face it, who wouldn't want to take advantage of this during the summer when mosquitos make life impossible?

Due to the pleasantly calming aroma of the burned herbs, smudging can also be seen as a form of aromatherapy. Inhaling soothing herbal fragrances foster neurotransmitter modulation in the brain. Neurotransmitters are chemicals needed to transport and process information throughout the nervous system. In other words, smudging enables your nervous system to intake, process, and transmit information more effectively.

Another reason smudging with certain herbs purifies space is that the smoke neutralizes *positive ions* (not to be confused with positive vibes, which are also beneficial). Positive ions are particles that tie down energy, making it unavailable for harnessing or manipulation. You foster positive ion accumulation in the air when you're angry or stressed. It starts with the positively charged air you release from your lungs, which permeates the energy in the room. Then, the room's air becomes stagnant due to the prevailing number of positive ions. After a while, you start feeling lethargic and can't seem to embrace positivity no matter how hard you try. Herbs used in smoke cleansing can make negative ions from positive ones, effectively purging the atmosphere from the latter.

The space-cleansing benefits of smudging can come in handy when moving into a new home or when negativity has been a long-term inhabitant of your home or office. For example, if you had an abusive or disruptive relationship with a difficult person you lived with - and they've moved out of your shared space - smudging the property could ensure all the negativity they invited into it leaves too.

Smoke cleansing can also be an efficient way to purify objects. If you work with magical or spiritual tools, regularly smudging them can significantly enhance their power and effectiveness. Even cleaning everyday objects has beneficial effects on the energetic makeup of their environment. This is particularly true for antique items, which have probably accumulated a plethora of different energies during their lifetime. Simply passing a lit smudge stick over them will ensure their aura can't negatively affect you, your space, or those around you.

Another superb idea for smudging objects is using herbal smoke on presents you intend to give. By infusing your gifts with a soothing aroma of herbs, you're passing on their benefits to the recipients, allowing them to fill their space and person with positivity.

Ethical Considerations Regarding the Practice of Smudging

Modern spiritual and new-age shamanic practitioners often boast about smudging being a closed practice, indicating that its best used by those who understand its cultural origins. While acting contrary to this would imply that the practice has become an example of cultural appropriation (when one culture takes elements from another without permission or understanding the original context), there is much more to this topic.

Nevertheless, to use smudging respectfully, you must approach the practice with greater sensitivity, respect, and understanding.

More and more non-Natives (including influential celebrities) are showcasing the use of this practice for their own spiritual explorations without fully understanding its history and cultural significance. Smoke cleansing can be seen as inappropriate if done without courteous respect for the tradition. That being said, it's crucial to note that not everyone practices smudging this way out of disrespect. They simply see its spiritual benefit. However, even if you have the best intentions, you can cause harm if you don't properly respect the traditions surrounding the practice. When engaging in smudging, it's fundamental to take time to research its history and understand its significance within the original contexts. Doing this helps prevent the practice from becoming cultural appropriation.

Cultural appropriation often entails adopting symbols from other cultures or attempting to pass off traditional practices as your own. This happens because many people learn about smudging from non-research-based books, TV shows, and movies rather than obtaining information from traditional sources. Consequently, they fail to gain knowledge of its spiritual significance and implications.

Another factor to consider is the respectful use of sacred plants and responsible material sourcing. These are both critical to promote sustainable and responsible use of herbs and to honor the cultural and spiritual traditions of Indigenous and Native American communities. The best way to source your material ethically is to use herbs growing in your area. Find out what plants grow near you and the benefits they can provide for spiritual cleansing.

Chapter 2: Identifying Negative Energy

As you may have realized by now, smudging is all about driving away the negative energy from a place or a living being, making space for positive energy to enter. But before you can do that, you need to be certain that the energy contained in the object is negative. How can you point out that someone or something is surrounded by negative energy? It is easy to make the identification once you get the hang of the process. To make understanding the intriguing specifics of the method easier still, here are the fundamentals of sensing and recognizing energy itself.

Smudging is about driving away the negative energy from a space or living being – and making space for positive energy to enter."

What Is Energy?

In physics, energy is nothing more than a force that can be exerted to perform work. But the same physics has also given mankind the direct relationship between matter and energy. Remember Albert Einstein's famous equation, $E=mc^2$ ("E" is energy, and "m" stands for mass or matter)? Thus, energy isn't just an abstract, invisible entity that grants force to objects. It is a very real thing that can be felt all around you.

Energy was present before the birth of the universe, and it will remain long after the world is no more. In its raw state, it is pure, powerful, and all-encompassing. It cannot be seen or felt if you don't know what you are looking for. Different forms of energy vibrate at different frequencies. And the most important form of energy is thoughts. They vibrate at different frequencies too.

What Is Energy Vibration and Movement?

The vibration of energy is governed by the Law of Vibration. It states that all forms of energy are constantly vibrating. No energy is ever at rest, for if it is, then it is energy no longer but a void of nothingness, sort of a vacuum. The frequency of vibration determines the kind of energy it is.

Frequencies that are alike tend to resonate with each other, merging together to form a greater kind of that energy. They travel across the universe, continuing to merge with energies that vibrate at their frequency – ever accumulating, ever-growing. This concept is easier to understand with an energy body instead of a physical body.

Energy Body and Its Significance

An energy body (alternatively called an Astral body) is nothing but a physical body as seen in the form of pure energy. It's like looking at your body in a different spectrum, like infrared. It is said that your energy body is around five inches larger than your physical body. It comprises various energy centers (Chakras) and energy channels (Meridians). Chakras ensure the healthy function of your physical body, whereas Meridians are responsible for circulating the absorbed energy throughout the body.

In the energy body, your thoughts are visible fragments of your mind, and you can feel the frequency of their vibration. When you think about something for the first time, a fragment of that thought is generated in your energy body. Your mind sends out the frequency of that thought's vibrations into the universe. But to manifest that thought into something real and visible in the physical sense, you need to establish energetic harmony.

What Is Energetic Harmony?

In simple words, energetic harmony is a balance between different kinds of energy. Take musical harmony, for instance. Just like different notes, tempos, pitches, etc., are played in perfect sync to form a musical harmony, different kinds and frequencies of energy come together to give rise to an energetic harmony.

This fantastic music of the universe can either be profoundly soothing or insanely chaotic. It entirely depends upon the keys that you play to achieve that harmony. These keys are nothing but your thoughts. If you play the right keys (read: think positive thoughts), like thinking about cheering up your neighbors or giving a percentage of your salary to charity, then the vibrations generated will resonate with other similar vibrations in the universe, bringing about an amazingly positive energetic harmony.

On the other hand, if you play the wrong keys (read: think negative thoughts), like feeling jealous of your friend's success or planning revenge on an enemy, then those vibrations will merge only with other similar vibrations, giving rise to a cacophony of negative energetic harmony (read: utter chaos).

That is what negative energy looks and feels like, and it is what will be identified in this chapter. But before getting to the process of identifying that energy, it is important to understand the concept of negative energy in depth.

What Is Negative Energy?

In its raw form, energy is neither positive nor negative. It just is. Your thoughts make the energy lean toward the polar extremes. Bad thoughts will generate negative energy in a space or an individual. It always starts off small. In the initial stages, an infinitesimal part of your surroundings will be converted to negative energy.

This part will attract other similar negative energies from the universe, growing in proportion with the multiple merges until it eventually occupies the entire space, pushing out the neutral and positive energies.

That is when smudging comes into the picture to make space for positivity. Neutral energy can be converted to negative from three possible sources.

1. **Negative Self**

    Do you tend to dwell on your regrets rather than thinking about your promising future? Do feelings of jealousy eat you up on the inside? Do you hate people more than you feel love for them? Is your mind often occupied with negative thoughts? If you answered even one of these questions in the affirmative, then you have negative energy within and around you.

    It may simply be a small dark patch in your energy body or a radiating aura of negativity. Either way, your own dark thoughts brought the rancid atmosphere to life.

2. **Negative People**

    It doesn't always have to be you who brings negative energy to your energy body. You don't have to be inherently negative. The energy that the people around you project can also affect your aura. Suppose you let the negativity of your family, friends, and acquaintances influence your thoughts. In that case, your negative energy is merging with theirs and expanding in your surroundings, leaving no place for positivity.

3. **Negative Surroundings**

    When you enter a space rife with negative energy, there is a high chance that it may seep into your positive/neutral energy body. It so happens that, sometimes, when you enter a room, a feeling of discomfort immediately creeps up on you. That is most probably because of the negative energy confined in it. It may start affecting your thoughts, generating gloomy images of the past in your mind.

    Negative surroundings like that could turn out to be anything. It could be a place where you have had a bad encounter in the past, like a sports ground where you lost to the opposition. Or it could be a space you associate with negative occurrences, like a morgue.

In essence, negative energy is nothing but a collection of bad thoughts. The greater the number of bad thoughts confined in a space, the more negative energy it will contain. And often, it is not easily recognizable until it's too late – when the negativity entirely consumes your soul. It can be compared to cancer, curable when detected in the early stages but fatal if diagnosed late.

No need to fret, however. Here you will learn everything there is to know about identifying negative energy in its simplest, most infinitesimal forms so that you can detect it early and smudge the place before the negativity spreads out of control.

How to Identify Negative Energy

Now that you know what negative energy is and what it looks and feels like, identifying it won't be much of a problem. You may find it difficult initially, but once you get used to the process, it will become second nature to you. It's like learning how to ride a bike. You may fall a few times at first, but eventually, you will get it right. You just need to keep a lookout for the signs.

What to Look for While Identifying Negative Energy?

The line between right and wrong, good and bad, positive and negative, is sometimes blurred. You can overlook something that is commonly considered to be wrong but may be right for you. These apparently good things may eventually lead to something decidedly bad, like some innocent prank gone wrong. Hence, avoiding the gray areas and focusing on definite negativity while identifying negative energy is better. Here's what you may consider looking for.

- Incessant health problems for you and in the people around you
- Repeated arguments and bad vibes between two or more individuals
- Unsolvable work-related issues that keep piling up
- An overall lack of success
- A general feeling of lethargy
- Blanking out often and at odd times
- A constant feeling of unease and/or anxiety
- Continued lack of sleep, at least for a week
- Unusual occurrences around the place that cannot be rationally explained

As you can see, the only point that isn't inherently negative is the last one. Those unusual occurrences may also lead to something good. But it's always better to be safe than sorry. And anyway, smudging removes only negative energy from a place and keeps the positivity. So, if the rationally inexplicable happenings lead to something positive, their source won't be removed through smudging.

You can identify negative energy using one or all three mediums: the people, yourself, or the environment. Ask the following questions to determine the presence of negative energy.

- **Identification through People**

    Is there a general sense of animosity between people? Are they often on edge? Do full-blown arguments break out from the tiniest of disagreements? Are they often down with the flu? Is someone nearly always afflicted with some health issues every second of every day? Has nobody found success in their undertakings despite working hard? Does nobody seem to muster the strength to work hard?

- **Identification through Yourself**

    This is probably the easiest way to identify negative energy. After all, you know yourself better than you know others.

    Do you often tend to lose focus on the task at hand? Does your mind go blank for long periods (zero-state of thinking)? Do you tend to dwell more on negative thoughts than on positive ones? Are you often sick with various kinds of health problems, one after the other, like fever one week followed by constipation the next, and so on? Do you suffer from the same health issue far longer than usual?

    Is your mind occupied with positive or negative thoughts while trying to sleep? Are you often so critical of something that you tend to lose sight of its virtue? Do you find yourself complaining about the smallest of things? Do you overthink and overanalyze your mistakes instead of focusing on the good parts or solutions?

- **Identification through the Environment**

    This is more of a comparative method than an identification medium in itself. Simply ask yourself the above questions in different environments. For instance, is your mind occupied with negative thoughts at home? Then go to your friend's place and see if those negative thoughts still haunt you. If they don't, then it's likely that the negative energy exists in your home. But if they do follow you, then there is a high probability that the negative energy lies within you.

Alternatively, are your colleagues in a constant state of agitation at your workplace? But do they seem happy and content when you go out for drinks? Then the negative energy is present at your workplace. However, if your colleagues are still agitated during the evening out, then it's likely that negative energy is present within the group.

Another way to determine the existence of negative energy in the environment is to go with your instincts or gut feelings. Do you suddenly feel uncomfortable after entering a room? Do goosebumps start creeping up your spine when visiting an unknown place?

Granted, these questions are often hard to answer if you are just starting out on your identification journey, especially the last ones. You may fail to correctly recognize negative energy for what it is initially. But know that it is a process of trial and error. It's perfectly okay if you keep failing at first, but as soon as you can correctly identify the presence of negative energy, you will rarely fail again.

There is another easier way of identifying negative energy, and that is by analyzing emotions. Negative energy produces negative emotions. Thus, you need to watch out for the frequency of the following emotions in yourself or in others around you.

- **Anger**

    Do small things make you or others angry? Let's say that you're getting ready to go to work, and your younger brother has misplaced your favorite shirt. Is your first instinct to lash out at him instead of calmly asking him about it?

- **Irritation**

    Do you often find yourself irritated by the smallest of things? For example, you are trying to get some work done. Suddenly, someone enters your cubicle without knocking. Does that annoy you?

- **Depression**

These days, depression has become one of the most commonly felt negative emotions in the world, so much so that it is categorized as a medical illness. Are you feeling utter hopelessness? Has sadness enveloped your heart? On a happy occasion, do you find yourself brooding in a corner?

- **Fear**

At times, it is okay to feel fear, like arachnophobes feel when they spot a spider, or when you're witnessing/experiencing something horrific, or if you're watching a horror movie. But if you're afraid almost all the time, then that may be the result of negative energy.

- **Anxiety**

Anxiety and fear often go hand in hand. Whenever you're anxious about undertaking a task, you probably fear botching that task. Does something as simple as getting out of bed and going about your day make you anxious? Are you often nervous about doing little things, like talking to your neighbors or watching the news?

- **Guilt**

You feel guilty when you do something that goes against your moral code. And that is usually good because it keeps your behavior in check. But when you start dwelling on that guilt, so much so that it overwhelms you, that is probably due to negative energy.

- **Envy**

Feelings of jealousy are quite common among humans. If someone takes what is yours, rightfully so or otherwise, it is normal to feel a bit of envy. But if you're consumed by that emotion, then it will give rise to other negative emotions. And you will eventually be surrounded by negative energy.

- **Contempt**

There is a very thin line separating pride and contempt. Feeling proud of your accomplishment? Good. But do you look down on those who cannot accomplish what you did? That's contempt, and it is definitely a negative emotion. You may be steeped in negative energy if you often feel contemptuous toward others.

- **Hate**

  They say that without hate, there can be no love. But it doesn't mean that you should let hate govern or dictate your actions. Do you tend to hate people without rhyme or reason? Is your first instinct after meeting someone new to hate them? Do even the good actions of your fellow humans generate hatred in your heart?

These are the most common emotions you can easily use to identify negative energy. Many other emotions imply the presence of negative energy, like shame, misery, loneliness, disgust, etc., but people don't usually express these. Even you may not realize your loneliness unless someone points it out!

What NOT to Look for While Identifying Negative Energy

Now that you know the signs to identify negative energy, it is time to learn what to avoid taking that knowledge into consideration. On rare occasions, it is easy to mistake something positive for negative energy. At other times, it is easier still to blame negative energy when you are experiencing the direct consequences of your actions.

- **Fleeting Negativity**

  Is it the first time in a while that you were angry at someone? Have your colleagues been arguing only for a while? Did your health problems last no longer than a day or two? These may not be instances of negative energy. When the problems fester and keep piling up over several days, only then could it be a cause for concern.

- **Wrong Action for the Right Reasons**

  When you notice someone displaying a negative emotion, try to figure out why they feel that way. It may be that a person is angry because they saw some injustice being done. You may be feeling anxious because you want to get the task done perfectly. Your actions or emotions may be negative, but if your reasons for doing/displaying them are positive, then you may avoid negative energy.

- **Subjectively Negative**

Is it really something negative that you're observing, or is it only a negative instance to you? Take meat-eating, for example. You may be a vegan who firmly believes that non-vegetarians are what is wrong with the world. However, most of the world's population (more than 80%) consumes meat and animal products; thus, eating meat isn't a negative trait in the grand scheme of things.

To summarize the techniques of identifying negative energy, you should always know the signs to look for and to avoid. Negative energy is generated through negative afflictions, thoughts, emotions, or occurrences. You can point out the presence of negative energy through three different mediums, namely, yourself, the people around you, and your surroundings. Remember that emotions are the best and easiest way to identify negative energy in a place or person.

Chapter 3: Before You Start

Although a simple smudging ritual consists of easy steps and requires just a few supplies, the technique's effectiveness depends on some preliminary arrangements. In addition to finding and arranging a sacred space to carry out the smudging process, you also need to clear your mind, ground yourself and set the intentions in your special space. This can include creating an altar or simply setting up the smudging space with the necessary supplies.

Creating a sacred space is an essential part of the process that should not be skipped if you want the process to be effective. Setting the intentions for the ceremony is also a crucial step, as it helps create a spiritually charged atmosphere. Once this is done, the respective invocations are said, and the smudging process begins.

However, before learning about that process, you must know how to prepare your space and *when* to perform this technique. This chapter will include a guide to the preliminary groundwork required for smudging rituals, followed by instructions on when to practice these rituals.

Creating an Altar

An altar is a space designated to honor the spirits, universe, and other divine beings.⁴⁶

Smudging is a deeply spiritual process, and, as with any other divine process, it requires a sacred space where it can be performed. This is where an altar comes in, which, in essence, is a space designated to honor the spirits, universe, and other divine beings. It's a place where you make offerings to the spirit world and express gratitude for your blessings. If you have any experience with other esoteric practices, you'll know the significance altars are usually given.

On the other hand, if you're just starting out on your spiritual journey, the thought of creating an altar may seem intimidating at first. However, it's a creative process that helps you express your inner soul. In fact, on a subconscious level, any time you place beautiful pieces on your mantel, table center, or shelf, you're essentially creating an altar. In this sense, you're already creating little altars around your home whenever you group together objects you love.

Your smudging altar can either be generic or specific to the intent of your ritual. For instance, if your intention is to attract better health or welcome love, your altar should be decorated keeping this in mind. You may think altars are just decorative spaces, but they're so much more. They need regular energetic movement and care, so when you do create an altar, it becomes your responsibility to care for it daily. The key to creating the most energy-filled altars is to be specific and conscious when you're setting it up. For instance, if you're creating an altar for spiritual protection, you must decorate it with crystals and other spiritual tools associated with protection and set the intentions accordingly. As a result, your sacred space will develop the power needed to complete your goals.

The best part about creating an altar is that no specific rules are involved. Your altar is a sacred space that is your own and should be an expression of your intentions and energy. This means the more empowered you are while creating your altar, the more power will be imbued in it. If you're an absolute beginner, you can follow a set of guidelines to make the process easier for you. Here are some steps you should consider:

1. **The Area**

    Choose the area and surface of the altar in a place where you will not get disturbed. This does not specifically have to be a designated altar space and can be as simple as your bedside table or the windowsill. You can even use extra space on your bookcase as your smudging altar or create one on the fireplace mantel. Of course, this doesn't mean you can't set up a separate space with a table prepared just for this purpose. Wherever you decide to set up this stage, you should keep in mind that smudging produces smoke that needs a place to escape. Your room should have windows and doors for ample ventilation. Remember to keep these open when you're performing the smudging ritual.

2. **The Theme**

    If you have a particular intention for which you need to perform the smudging process, it's best to design your altar according to that theme. For instance, you may need more clarity in life or desire more energy or vitality. You may want to express or attract love and create powerful relationships or practice gratitude for the blessings in your life. Whatever the case, you can create an altar designed specifically with that intention in mind. The most common altar themes are love, gratitude, and connection.

3. **Spiritual Tools**

   When you're performing smudging, you'll find that the space will be surrounded by a lot of spiritual energy. You can use energy enhancers and other spiritual tools to contain and enhance this energy near the altar. For instance, you can use a piece of fabric or a tray as the foundation of energy. On it, you can put candles, crystals, flowers, specific images, sculptures, and any special items you find in nature, like seashells, stones, etc. You will also want to designate a space on your altar to keep your smudging tools.

   There should be a beautiful, restful space where you can put your smudge stick or palo santo in between smudging sessions. Other smudging tools can also be displayed on this altar. These can include smudging fans, feathers, abalone shells, etc. When these tools are kept on your smudging altar, they'll be kept safe and organized and accumulate power from their surroundings. Crystals are usually the most popular choice for altar setup, as they help you tap into the energy of your smudge tools. More on crystals in a later chapter.

Setting the Intentions

Every type of smudging ritual follows almost the same order, which starts with setting the intentions of the process. After the intention, spiritual energy is invoked, and the actual smudging process follows. Setting the intentions for a smudging process is one of its most essential steps. Without an intention, all kinds of energies are being attracted toward your space, which you want to avoid at all costs. Setting intentions does not have to be a super complicated process, where you use numerous tools or only speak in confusing tones and flowery language! It can be as simple as lighting a candle and speaking out your intention for the process, like, *"My intent for this ritual is to get rid of all the negative energy in my bedroom."* If you know any prayers or mantras, you can also use those to set the intentions of the ritual.

Having a clear picture of your intention and expressing it at the beginning of the smudging ritual is the first step in the process and should not be neglected. It's an empowering act of trust, focus, and surrender. So, take a few moments before any ritual to clarify your intent. Let the universe know what energies you want to invite into your life.

Gathering Supplies

The process of smudging and purifying your energy is surprisingly simple. In fact, you only need a smudge stick, a candle, a charcoal tablet, and two medium-sized bowls (one of them should be used to catch the flaming ashes falling from your smudge stick, while the other one should hold the smudge stick once you've finished the ritual). Both of these should be fireproof – try using ceramic bowls instead of plastic ones. After completing the process, you can fill the second bowl with sand so the smudge stick will be extinguished automatically. If you don't have access to sand, you can use salt in its place. However, try to avoid using water to put the flames out because this can create a harsh type of energy. Your smudging supplies should be kept on the altar you have created.

You can also add a smudging fan or feather to your supplies if you want to add to the value of the process. This is particularly helpful if you use sage bunches instead of the whole stick. Various beautiful smudging fans are available in stores and online; making them yourself is even better.

You can practice smudging in your home with sage, palo santo, or other herbs in two ways. The traditional method uses a smudge stick, while the lesser-used technique burns loose leaves in a fireproof bowl. If you don't have much experience with smudging rituals, it's best to stick to a smudge stick or sage branch rather than burning loose leaves. This is a comparatively straightforward process and does not require particular skills. You'll only have to worry about the ashes falling from the smudge stick and the risk of starting a fire. However, this problem can be easily remedied by keeping a bowl under the stick while smudging your space. Still, if you're nervous about the process, you should start by using just a few branches instead of the whole stick for the process. This will help you become more confident while you develop your smudging abilities. To get the branches, just unbundle a smudge stick and use a few of its branches to smudge your space.

The second option takes a bit more work than the traditional one, so it's best that you start with the easier one first and gradually move up to it. For this option, you will need a fireproof container to burn the loose herbs right inside the bowl. Although some people prefer to use abalone shells for this purpose, it is not recommended as they are not entirely fireproof. Instead, you can use those shells to display the sage leaves on your altar and use a simple ceramic bowl to burn them. Or, you could use abalone shells to catch the ashes falling from the burning leaves during smudging. Place some sand at the base of your fireproof container, followed by a charcoal tablet, and then put the leaves in place. Like smudge sticks, the loose-leaf blends also contain various herbs, including lavender, white sage, cedar, rose petals, juniper, and other herbs. You can either get a pre-made bundle of herbs or make it yourself.

When to Smudge

While there are no restrictions about when and where you can perform a smudging ritual, certain times are more suitable than others, depending on the intention. If you've never smudged your space before, now is a good time to start because your house has probably accumulated a ton of negative energy over the years. Even if you think you live in the most harmonious house, with the most positive interactions among your family, human energy creates a significant amount of energetic residue, similar to how dust accumulates in your home daily.

Regular smudging is a good habit, just like drinking a cup of tea in the morning or performing your workout routine. When you make tea for yourself every morning, you go through the movements of the process and take a moment to connect with yourself. This becomes a cherished ritual that is incomparable to any other activity. The feelings of calm and peacefulness are more about the rhythm of the ritual than the tea itself, and it is exactly the same when you establish another ritual.

Once you've developed the intuitive ability to be aware of the energy around you, you'll know exactly when you need to perform the smudging process. The need for spiritual cleansing can be a result of various things. For instance, a family conflict or some items you recently brought home, etc.

Life Situations That Smudging Can Improve

When your family is struggling, your space likely gets contaminated with negative emotions and energies. This is the best time to do a smudging ritual. You'll automatically become aware of the negative energies plaguing your house when you learn of this type of recent event. Smudging at times like this helps clear the energy after an argument and eliminates the tension between family members. You can also practice smudging if you or one of your family members are going through a difficult time in their personal life, at work, or at school, or is facing anything emotionally challenging. This practice can help you deal with heavy emotions like anxiety, depression, sadness, fear, and mental fatigue.

The low, stagnant, negative energies accumulating in a space can make it hard to breathe and make things worse for you. This is why smudging is essential, not just some spiritual voodoo people practice. The cleansing carried out by this sacred ritual helps you clear the way for a deeper, clearer connection to your inner self and the people around you. Think of it like this. Living in a house filled with negative energy is like trying to gaze at a beautiful garden through dirty windows. You cannot see anything clearly, even though the pretty flowers are right outside. To see the full beauty of the garden, you'd have to clean the dirty windows. Similarly, when left unattended, negative energies can gather in the deepest parts of your life and ultimately distort your view. Everyone is deeply connected by the energy of their homes, this is the place where you spend most of your time, and therefore, your aura is interconnected with your home's energy. When you clear and clean the energy around you, you're doing the same for the energy within you. So, whether you practice a simple or complicated version of a smudging ritual, it will help keep the energy in your home protected and pure.

Challenging Situations and Events That Would Require Smudging Your Home Include:

- A big fight
- Verbal or physical abuse
- Having rude guests
- The death of a family member
- Financial trouble
- An accident

- Relationship problems
- Illnesses

Whenever you're going through a tough time in your life, smudging can help clear out negativity and provide you with the support to get through the situation easily. Think of it in this way. Not clearing your house of negative energies is like eating breakfast on unwashed dinner plates. Would you eat anything served on a dirty plate? Most homes are filled to the brim with unwanted, negative energy, like the grime on these dirty dishes, which makes it very hard for people to be happy and healthy in these heavily toxic homes.

Many people emphasize the importance of decluttering a home to create a harmonious space, but they rarely talk about the energetic clearing of negative residues and imprints left in one's home. In fact, if you feel like there's ever-growing clutter inside your house that's proving impossible to clear, try to do a smudging ritual, and you'll see a notable difference in the energy flow of your home, making it easier for you to declutter. Smudging can also help with brighter instances, like when you're starting a new relationship, starting a new project, or moving to a new home. In these cases, smudging creates an environment filled with positive energy, which attracts all good things into your life.

Best Times of the Day to Smudge

Regarding energy cycles, a day has the same four cycles as the whole year. It moves from the depth of night (winter) to the morning (spring) to noon (summer), and finally, to the evening (autumn). This cycle is why so many people prefer to perform their smudging rituals in the early morning. There's something so calming yet invigorating about an early-morning smudging practice that starts your day on a most positive note. The best time to practice smudging in the morning is between 5 AM to 7 AM, during which time you can open up the energy channels from the universe and bring positive energy into your life. This habit of smudging is similar to smudging during the spring equinox. Plus, the morning practice helps you center your energy and makes you feel calmer. It opens you up to the possibilities of the day and prepares you to receive all kinds of positive energies.

Another good time to practice smudging during the day is between 11 AM and 1 PM. However, this doesn't seem as great as early morning smudging energy; it is said to be the most potent energy of the day – just like summer solstice is the best time for spiritual rituals. You can also enhance the effectiveness of your smudging rituals by incorporating the energy of seasonal and moon cycles. Working in harmony with the world's natural rhythms adds an energetic boost to your smudging sessions. However, you should note that considering these cycles is not necessary for your daily or weekly smudging routines. Using seasonal and moon cycles is especially helpful for larger smudging rituals when you have a specific intention in mind.

To determine the best timing for your ritual, start by clearly defining your intention. Are you looking to release and let go of negative energy, or are you seeking to invite specific positive energy into your life? Every smudging ritual involves clearing away negativity and welcoming positive energy. However, having a well-defined intent for a specific smudging ritual will help direct the energy most beneficially. Aligning the timing of your smudging with your intent will give your ritual an extra boost.

This chapter has covered the essential preparations required before engaging in the smudging process. Before embarking on this ancient practice, it is crucial to ensure proper preparations are undertaken to create a harmonious and sacred environment. By embracing these preparations, you can honor the ancient smudging traditions and create a sacred space for spiritual growth and healing. Smudging is a powerful tool for clearing negative energies, restoring balance, and inviting positive vibrations into your lives.

Chapter 4: Herbs, Resins, and Oils

The variety of herbs, oils, and resins used for smudging seems unlimited, with herbs ranging from the commonly used ones, including sage, lavender, and juniper, to the less popular options like cedarwood, vervain, and rosemary. Your choice of products depends on different influences, but mainly on what's available in your area. You can choose to use just one herb or create a smudge stick with a combination of different herbs. This is where your intuition will guide you, and some guidelines will give you the basic framework for selecting the products to use in a smudging ritual. This chapter is all about selecting herbs, resins, and oils for different types of smudging routines. It will also include a step-by-step guide to using resins, essential oils, and other products to practice a smudging ritual.

Choice of Herbs

Although there are no specific rules when making herb combinations for smudging, you should know what were considered the four sacred medicines in Native American traditions - tobacco, cedar, white sage, and sweetgrass - are never mixed. Other than this one rule, there are no limitations. Below are the most popular herbs, along with their specific properties. Your choices primarily depend on these properties and how they align with your intentions.

1. Cedar

The cedar tree.⁴⁷

The cedar tree is one of the oldest trees on this planet; as such, it is potent, full of spiritual energy, and majesty. This herb has been associated with protection and cleansing and used for smudging and other spiritual purification processes by many Native American tribes. Cedar is considered to be a powerful healing herb and a guardian spirit that protects your home.

2. Juniper

Juniper is an ancient herb with strong properties of protection and blessings.⁴⁸

Dating just as far back as the cedar tree, juniper is an ancient herb with strong properties of protection and blessings. Many tribes have used it for protection rituals and to attract abundance and blessings into the home. The smudging energy of juniper can also calm and purify your space and brings positive energy to an otherwise negatively charged space.

3. Lavender

Lavender has been used in smudging rituals for a long time. As you may know, lavender has soothing properties and is used in many natural herbal remedies. However, did you know it's also a very popular smudging herb, providing a sense of calm and clarity? It helps relieve stress and provides your space with sweet, nourishing energy. Burning lavender is also preferred as an after-smudging ritual to form a final protective shield around your space.

Lavender has soothing properties and is used in many natural herbal remedies.⁴⁹

4. Pine

Pine helps deepen your breathing and makes your head feel clearer and more focused.[50]

Pine has a deeper effect on people rather than the space itself. It can help deepen your breathing and make your head feel clearer and more focused. It grounds and centers you. This herb is used to help bring forgiveness during difficult situations.

5. Sage

Sage helps bring clarity, peacefulness, and protection.[51]

Sage is the most popular herb for smudging rituals. When you hear the word smudging, the first herb that comes to mind is sage or white sage. This herb brings clarity, peacefulness, and protection. You can also use it to invoke the blessings of the divine universe. In addition to white sage, some other varieties exist, including black sage, purple sage, and blue sage. In fact, there are almost 300 varieties of sage. However, they're not all commonly used for smudging purposes.

6. Sweetgrass

Sweetgrass, another popular smudging herb used for centuries, provides all sorts of benefits. Its vanilla-like aroma evokes a sense of trust, clarity, and peace. It resembles a sweet, nourishing, gentle presence, often associated with motherly energy. Native people call it the hair of Mother Earth. Traditionally, sweetgrass smudge sticks are created by braiding three strands of this herb, each representing kindness, love, and honesty.

7. Rose

Rose petals are usually used in combination with lavender to create beautifully scented smudge sticks. Rose petals add a touch of graceful energy and attract love, healing, and harmony. They can also be combined with rosemary, thyme, and wild sage.

8. Rosemary

According to ancient smudging traditions, rosemary has the power to protect your space from negativity while also cleansing it. Since it is a very energizing herb, it's usually combined with sage and other herbs for the best results.

9. Thyme

Thyme is frequently used in conjunction with rosemary to purify and safeguard. It also enhances vitality, courage, and confidence while soothing the energy of sadness.

Although most combinations work well, you should listen to your intuition when making smudging combinations. Although you're encouraged to make herb combinations, it is suggested that you do not use too many herbs in a single combination as that can mix up their properties.

Burning Sacred Resin

Burning resins is another ancient ritual, which is very similar to smudging, if not even more powerful. Sacred resins are obtained from healing trees – the most popular ones being copal, frankincense, and myrrh. Each of these has unique properties, and at the same time, they provide almost the same benefits. Frankincense has protecting, cleansing, and uplifting properties, myrrh is used to clear confusion and align a person to the sweetness of their heart, and copal is used to clear the mind, eliminate any energy blocks, and attract positive energy into your life.

All three of these resins have in common their ability to cleanse and protect, which opens up the way for positive energy. Whether you want to attract love, abundance, inner peace, or better health, these resins can be used to provide the same properties as burning herbs. These resins are usually combined to make up a more potent solution, and other herbs are sometimes added to the mix. As with all herbs, oils, and resins, setting your intention before the process is essential.

Although resin is a better option for smudging if you don't like the smell of burning herbs, it also requires some extra work. You must put in some time and effort to gather the necessary supplies. You should try this, especially if you've never done it before, because the fragrance of burning resin is wonderful! The aroma is said to connect you with the ancient roots of this universe and bring out deep emotional feelings. Many find the process to be incredibly grounding and, at the same time, deeply mystical. These are the supplies you'll need for burning sacred resins:

- A fireproof, heat-resistant bowl
- A bit of sand to place in the bowl
- Incense charcoal

A pair of tongs Your choice of sacred resin A candle Here are the six steps for burning sacred resin:

1. Gather your supplies and keep them in a place within reach. Make sure they're on an even surface to avoid a mess. Your altar would be a great place to start.
2. Fill the fireproof container with sand as you would with a regular smudging ritual.
3. Light the candle and hold the charcoal on top of the flame using the tongs.
4. Keep it there until it lights up or becomes reddish. Once that happens, place the charcoal on top of the sand in the fireproof bowl.
5. Make sure the charcoal is heated evenly, and it should change color. If it doesn't, try to heat the edges before you place it inside the bowl.

6. Once the charcoal forms a layer of gray ash when placed on the sand, you'll know it's ready to burn resin.
7. Finally, place a small amount of resin on top of the hot charcoal and enjoy its fragrance.
8. You can keep adding small amounts of resin after it melts.

If you're just a beginner with resin smudging or even regular smudging, it's best not to move the bowl around too much on your first few attempts. Simply place it on an even surface where there's no risk of it falling. After you've become more accustomed to the ritual, you can try moving it around the room and to and from different rooms. However, place the fireproof container on top of a small tray to keep it stable.

Do not use abalone shells instead of fireproof bowls, no matter how aesthetically pleasing or ritual-like it looks. The shell is not fireproof and will get damaged. You could instead opt for censers. There's a wide range of censers available in the market, from the huge ones you see in churches and temples to the smaller ones used in homes worldwide.

You may struggle a bit with burning resin at the beginning. For instance, the charcoal may not light up easily or uniformly. However, with some trial and error, you will get the hang of the process, no matter how complicated it may sound at first.

Liquid Smudging

Liquid smudging is the easiest way to smudge without having to go through too many steps. Although the effects of this type of smudging are not the same as traditional smudging rituals, since it lacks the fire element, you will be creating a significant change in your home's energy when you practice liquid smudging. The process involves using a mixture of essential oils in pure water, the most popular combination being palo santo and white sage. You'll also find a variety of other mixes containing a range of essential oils on the market, or you can even make them yourself. In contrast with traditional smudging, you'll find various options for oils and liquid mixtures since this option is becoming increasingly popular, with most people opting for this low-effort smudging alternative.

The best thing about this technique is its portability; you can take it anywhere with you without worrying about fire safety. Plus, it's a quick process as compared to regular smudging, and it does not create smoke. So, you can even use it in your workplace, car, or hotel room. Even if you don't want to shift completely to liquid smudging, you can still opt for it sometimes while you're traveling or for a quick fix. You don't have to pick a single option and can choose multiple smudging techniques to incorporate into your routine, be it traditional, liquid, or other kinds of smudging rituals.

Natural Incense

The art of making incense is an ancient craft that has been carried out for spiritual purposes all over the world. These powerful solutions are created by following complex recipes and formulas for various spiritual rituals originating from ancient Egypt, Nepal, India, Tibet, and Japan. Since this practice has become very popular these days, many low-quality incense products are being sold. However, these products can easily be created by following a potent recipe of natural ingredients. Various incense products are available on the market, ranging from thin sticks that come in different lengths to small cones, rectangular bricks, incense coils, and even small, twisted ropes. There's even a wide variety of incense holders available in all shapes, sizes, colors, and materials.

If you've had any experience with burning incense, you're probably familiar with how frustrating those thin incense holders are. Once the incense sticks are done burning, there's ash scattered everywhere, creating a mess all around. Though you can opt for the wide incense holders, you can also try another, more spiritual technique of burning incense. You can create the base of the incense holder with some food material, like rice or grain, and place the incense sticks within this pile. This process not only helps spiritually cleanse your space, but the food also acts as an offering to the universe. Once the incense is done burning, you can mix its ashes with the grains or rice and place a new one in its place. In this way, you can also use several incense sticks simultaneously for a more purifying effect. If you want to select the best incense, buying it in person instead of ordering online is best. You'll have a direct experience with the fragrances of each product and find the product that is most suitable for you.

Essential Oils

The use of essential oils for smudging rituals is a favorite among many, especially since so many varieties and diffusers are present. Ultra-sonic diffusers are all the rage today. They use a cold mist to diffuse the essential oils into the air, so the scent is comparatively stronger than many other candle diffusers. But perhaps the best part is that this requires little or no effort from you. All you need to do is fill the diffuser with cold water and the essential oils of your choice and select the function and timings. This is the simplest way to energize your space and put positive energy into the environment through essential oils. Like liquid smudging, this process doesn't require you to burn anything and is thus missing the element of fire. So, while it can't be compared to traditional smudging rituals, it's still something that can be done on a daily basis.

The cleansing happens on a more subtle level, but it does have a considerable effect on the negative energy in your environment, not to mention the added benefit of your space smelling wonderful. Here are some of the most popular essential oils that are used for energy clearing. You can use a combination of these oils or simply stick to one at a time as you see fit. Remember that you might not react positively to the herbs used in each of these essential oils. Therefore, you should read any health disclaimers provided with these products.

- **Balsam Fir Oil**

  This pure essential oil has numerous uses, from relieving muscle tension to fighting infections and purifying the energy in any space. It has a refreshing, uplifting scent and helps balance the energy around you. By using this essential oil, you will feel your breathing get deeper and begin connecting with your inner wisdom.

- **Cedarwood Oil**

  A soothing, grounding, and warming herb oil, the woody scent of cedarwood oil is unmatched by any other and can be used to clear the energy of any negative vibrations. You can use it to imbue your space with protective and peaceful energy. Cedarwood itself is considered to be a symbol of abundance and wisdom.

- **Cypress Oil**

  In addition to having numerous medical benefits, Cyprus oil is also a popular choice for smudging rituals because of its clear and energizing fragrance. It is said to be a holistic solution for mind and body healing. Thus, it helps relieve one's anxiety, stress, and other mental issues. When you use this to smudge your space, your space will become filled with calm and vitality.

- **Eucalyptus Oil**

Another essential oil mainly popular for its medical benefits, including antibacterial, antiviral, anti-inflammatory, and antimicrobial properties, eucalyptus oil, is a frequently used ingredient for smudging rituals. It helps rejuvenate your energy, improve your memory, and help reduce the tension in your space, resulting in a clear, cleansed environment.

- **Frankincense Oil**

Frankincense originates from the resin of Boswellia carteri trees gathered from the wild. Its beautifying and purifying properties have been revered for centuries. Frankincense provides a comforting yet invigorating energy, elevating the atmosphere of any area and creating a profound sense of wellness. It is believed to enhance memory, alleviate inflammation, and support restful sleep if used consistently.

- **Juniper Berry Oil**

Juniper is renowned for its detoxifying and immune-boosting properties. In addition to its capacity to eliminate negativity and purify the surrounding air, juniper is highly soothing and helps you sleep better. The essence of juniper oil facilitates the dissipation of negative energy, providing a serene and safeguarded environment.

- **Lavender Essential Oil**

Undoubtedly, lavender stands out as not only the most popular but also one of the most versatile oils. Its remarkable cleansing, purifying, calming, and soothing properties harmonize with its revitalizing and energizing capabilities. Lavender, an adaptogenic herb, adapts to your energy level, delivering what is needed to restore balance, whether it requires activation or peace. For those new to essential oils, lavender is unquestionably the ideal choice to use in the beginning.

- **Palo Santo Oil**

Palo Santo embodies a unique duality of being uplifting yet grounding. Its exceptional power lies in its capacity to cleanse and purify by transforming low and negative energies within a space or an individual's energy field. Additionally, palo santo imparts a gentle and tranquil aura of peace. It is frequently employed in ceremonies to facilitate participants in achieving profound states of meditation and fostering a deep connection with the universe.

- **Peppermint Oil**

Peppermint oil has the remarkable ability to quickly alleviate tension within the body and the surrounding environment. Its cleansing and invigorating properties refresh the air, clear the mind, infuse the space with revitalizing energy, and evoke a sense of renewal and optimism. When creating essential oil mixtures, peppermint oil proves to be one of the finest additions, as it harmonizes seamlessly and enhances the effects of most air-purifying oils.

- **Pine Oil**

Pine oil has a fresh and empowering aroma accompanied by a calming and uplifting energy. Not only does it possess anti-inflammatory properties, but it also helps alleviate headaches and purifies the air by eliminating pathogens. Using pine oil can effectively transmute negative energy, creating a renewed sense of hope and rejuvenation.

- **Rosemary Oil**

Rosemary is a revitalizing essential oil that excels in purifying and energizing. It helps relieve stress, enhances mental clarity, and strengthens the immune system. As a member of the same family as lavender and sage, rosemary shares their remarkable ability to clear negative energy and instill a profound sense of peace.

- **White Sage Oil**

White sage is renowned for its revitalizing and purifying properties and its ability to cleanse negative energy. Its earthy aroma has a calming effect on the mind and can alleviate fears and anxiety. Additionally, white sage possesses antibacterial qualities that help fight infections. Throughout history, white sage has been widely used for its profound energetic and healing benefits.

Before you engage in smudging rituals with herbs, essential oils, and resins, consider a few disclaimers regarding fire safety and potential allergies. When working with open flames, exercise caution and ensure that you have a fire-safe container to catch any ashes or embers. Be mindful of your surroundings and keep flammable items away from harm. Additionally, remember that certain herbs and botanicals can trigger allergic reactions in some people. If you have known allergies or sensitivities, it's advisable to perform a patch test or consult a healthcare professional before using specific herbs or essential oils.

Chapter 5: How to Smudge

Smudging your home, items, and yourself with herbs will raise the vibrations of the object being cleansed.[53]

Now that you've thoroughly familiarized yourself with the background and basic tenets of smudging, you can examine the foundational steps and structure of a smudging ritual. This chapter provides general guidelines to follow. However, everyone will use a different technique. You'll also receive tips and instructions for an all-encompassing smoke bath and techniques for smudging objects.

The Basic Steps of Smudging

Smudging your home, items, and yourself with herbs will raise the vibrations of the object being cleansed. Below are the basics steps for smudging.

1. Setting an Intention

Although it's recommended that you establish an intention during the preparatory phase, it's not too late to do it as the first step of the smudging ritual itself. This can be done silently or aloud and as simply or elaborately as you want. Feel free to be as creative with your intention as you wish. Reasons for smudging can vary from wanting to clear negative energy to inviting positivity and blessings to connect with the higher self or nature to a desire to enjoy the beneficial essence of herbs in the air. Once you've set your intent, aim to keep it in focus during the entire ritual.

If you have trouble focusing on your intention, try using a focal point to enhance your concentration. For example, some practitioners find gazing at the smoke beneficial for keeping their concentration focused - a fundamental element during spiritual work. Others will visualize their intention. To do this, take a few moments to close your eyes and see all the negative energies in your space, self, or object released through the open windows and doors. Or, imagine white or gold light entering the fresh air and filling every corner of your space with its peacefulness.

Creating a mantra is another way to channel your intention and invite positive vibrations into your home. Create a simple mantra you can repeat to yourself, like "*This space/object/person is full of calmness and light,*" or "*All negativity be gone from here.*"

2. Invoking Spirit Guides, the Four Directions, or Higher Self

Invoking spiritual help is fundamental for purging rituals, especially when smudging for psychic protection and energy clearing. Choose who you want to summon and for what purpose, offer a prayer or affirmation of gratitude, or ask for protection from negative energies. You can also light a candle and focus on inviting your spirit guides into your space, then blow out the flame to signal the completion of this cleansing stage. The same applies when you want to tap into your higher self. Determine why you want to seek information for your inner spiritual entity and ask it to reveal itself.

Here is an example of a prayer you can use to invoke spirit guides:

"As I light this sacred herb, I ask you to join me,

To cleanse this (space/object/person/myself) and protect it from intrusions.

I ask you to help me heal and find strength and peace.

As the sacred herbs burn."

According to Native practitioners, the four cardinal directions have a unique significance in smudging. Consequently, it's fundamental to invoke them properly before the ritual. Here is a rundown of what the four directions represent:

- **East:** Associated with the new light of the day, which arises when the sun rises above the horizon in the morning. The East is believed to help manifest new beginnings and growth opportunities and channel wisdom.
- **South:** As the sun peaks, it emits most of its warmth. The south might also represent the earth, the most productive phase of the year, or a stage in someone's life.
- **West:** Attributed to maturity, the West is where the sun sets. As it dips below the horizon, the sun signals the end of the day. Similarly, this direction can signal the end of a journey or process.
- **North:** Connected to guidance and wisdom, the North is one of the quintessential directions. Encompassing the other three elements, the North represents the trials and tribulations one experiences during their life journey.

You can use different methods to honor the four elements, including the following prayer:

"I call on the spirits of this herb to ward off negativity from around me, seen or unseen.

I call on the spirit of the East, who brings air, to grant me peace and inspire me during this ritual.

I call on the spirit of the South, who brings fire, to empower and protect me.

I call on the spirit of the West, who brings water to cleanse and purify the object of the ritual.

I call on the spirit of the North, who brings the earth, to help me ground and enhance my intention.

I ask you all to look over me from above as I do my work.

I ask nature to guard me from below until all negativity is gone.

Thank you, elements and nature!"

3. Clearing

Clearing refers to the actual act of smudging oneself, the space, or the object that needs to be purged of negativity by waving the smudge stick around the area or object. Using a feather or fan helps to direct the smoke as needed. Alternatively, you can use your hands to move the smoke around. However, before you get to this, you must light the herbs. When using a smudge stick, hold one end over the flame until it flares up. Gently blow out the flame. Your plants should glow with a scintillation of orange light and have a steady stream of smoke emanating from them. Start steering the smoke around the object you are cleansing your space, yourself, or any item you wish to purge from negative energies.

4. Moving Mindfully

While smudging, it's essential to move mindfully and with intention. Don't worry - there isn't a right or wrong way to smoke cleanse your property or person. It's all about being aware of the energies. When purging a space, start at the main entry point, and move toward the corners. If purifying your entire home, take your time with the places you use often as well as the corners of rooms. Low vibrational energy often hides away in inaccessible areas. When cleansing yourself or an object, move slowly, pay attention to every detail, and spend extra time on the areas that feel weighed down with negativity.

Moving mindfully and with raised awareness is also a chance to make this practice more personal. Only you know what helps you focus and lets your energy flow. Everyone will approach smudging a little differently because they have distinct personalities. Accordingly, everyone requires different forms of mindfulness. If you try working mindfully in a certain way and it doesn't work, find something else that does allow you to clear your mind and work efficiently.

5. Closing the Ritual with Blessings

To bring a space cleansing ritual to a close, smudge around the four corners of the space, then seal the doorways with a prayer, mantra, or another tool (like salt or crystals) to keep any negative energy out and protect your sacred space. Or, you can go around the object or person you're cleansing, moving clockwise – or imagine a shield forming in the same direction if you're cleansing yourself. Express gratitude for the elements, the spiritual guides, and nature before extinguishing your smudge stick.

Take as long as you need to say thanks for all you have and the blessings you'll receive in the future. Thank the refreshed energy now residing in you, your tools, your space, or another person. As you reflect on your ritual, appreciate that negative energy is no longer blocking the flow of positivity, and embrace the opportunities this offers. When you're ready, take a deep breath and let your mind fill with your normal thoughts as you slowly return to your day-to-day activities.

Bonus: Techniques and Tips for Taking Smoke Baths and Smudging Objects

Cleansing objects, spaces, and people can be a fantastic way to reclaim the energy within them. Smudging can protect you from any negative vibes accumulated in them due to their interactions with negative energies. You can combine smoke-cleansing with other energy-boosting or exchanging methods like prayers, affirmations, sounds, essential oils, smudging with herbs or incense, visualization, or chanting. Below you will find step-by-step instructions and tips for cleansing any object, space, or person.

Smudge Ritual for Large Objects or Spaces

Cleansing bulkier items or pieces of property requires more energy. This ritual's recipe includes multiple dried herbs – depending on your needs, you can choose whether you want to use all or just some of them.

Ingredients:
- Basil
- Pine cones
- Cloves
- Lavender

- Rosemary
- Juniper
- Sweetgrass
- Cedar
- Palo santo
- Garden sage
- White sage

Instructions:

1. After opening windows, cleanse the object or space physically. Make sure it is free of debris and dust before you move on to smoke cleansing.
2. Select an intention (preferably in the form of prayer or affirmation) that resonates with your goals and recite it aloud while focusing on the object you are cleansing. For example, you can say something like:

    "I purge this object of all energy that doesn't belong here."

    "I want to fill this space/object with positive, soothing energy."

    "I am cleansing this space/object of negative energy to let in love and light."

3. Bind the herbs in a bundle and light them from one end until they give off smoke. Call on a spiritual helper you wish to channel and acknowledge the four directions.
4. Smudge an object by moving it above the smoke in a clockwise direction. As you smudge around the item, focus on releasing any negative energies that may have been left behind and inviting peace and love.
5. When cleansing a space, gently circulate the smoke with your hand, then move clockwise around the room to purify the desired area while repeating the intention.
6. Visualize the object/space surrounded by white light - symbolizing the renewed energy field now filled with positivity and protecting it from a
7. This is also optional, but you can chant your mantras or words of power that are meaningful to you while focusing on the

object/space. This will help raise its vibration and invite positive energy into your home. Or, you can keep focusing on your intention – do whatever helps manifest it more efficiently.

8. Finally, thank the spiritual source you worked with to help to cleanse this object or space and set a clear purpose for its future use.

Smudge Ritual for Smaller Items

If your practice involves regular interactions with negative influences, a banishing ritual for cleansing your tools is a must-have. Or, if you've just bought an antique item and aren't sure of its origins, smoke cleansing will prevent it from tainting your space with potentially disruptive energies. The following ritual should be performed whenever you feel an object has accumulated low vibrations.

Ingredients:

- White sage
- A candle
- Incense of your choice
- A ceramic dish for the incense
- Sweetgrass essential oil

Instructions:

1. After opening the windows, light a white candle, hold up the object, and say:

   "I banish all negativity from this object. It's not welcome here anymore."

2. Then, trace a circle around the candle with your fingers, moving clockwise. Likewise, burn the sage, moving clockwise around the object while thinking about the positive vibes you want to surround it and what you plan to do with the re-energized item.

3. As you do this, visualize a protective barrier forming around the object. Finally, blow out the candle and say:

   "Negativity, I release you from this object. You're free to go."

4. Put the sage on a dish, place it in the center of your workspace, and leave it to burn. It will clear your space and protect you from unwanted energies you freed from the object.

5. You can channel positive vibes toward the object now that you've released the negative energy. Sweetgrass can attract positive energy – so applying 10 to 20 drops of sweetgrass essential oil in a diffuser should do the trick. For optimal effects, do this every time you smudge.

A Smoke Bath for Improving Energy Flow

This smoke bath is designed to boost the energy flow through your entire chakra system. By taking it, your space and belonging will be cleansed of negative energies, and your physical, mental, and spiritual health will be restored.

Ingredients:

- Herbs or smudge stick of your choice (for example, sage, palo santo, or sweetgrass)
- An abalone shell (or, alternatively, a clay bowl)
- Matches
- A feather (optional if you do not want to use your hand)

Instructions:

1. To begin with, start by creating a soothing environment. Peace and tranquility will help you focus. This can be achieved with essential oils like lavender or chamomile, dimming the lights, playing soft music, burning incense, or any other measures that help create a calming atmosphere.
2. Think about the result you want to manifest. Be concise and honest when formulating the intention – as this is the most critical element of the ritual. It will also determine what other tools you need to support your purpose and work effectively.
3. Open your windows and keep your smudge stick or herb bundle smoking.
4. Next, take some deep breaths to relax your body and mind. You'll start by cleansing yourself – before moving on to objects and your environment. This requires intense focus.
5. Use a feather or your palm to waft the smoke around your body – from the top of your head to your feet.
6. Pay attention to your breathing – keep it slow and steady. If you wish, you can remain connected to your breathing by visualizing your intent.

7. As you breathe in, imagine all the negative energy entering your body, leaving you feeling relaxed and refreshed. As you breathe out, imagine releasing all this negativity away from you. Continue to do this until you're in a completely relaxed state.
8. Now it is time to open up and release all stagnant energy within yourself. To do this, recite the following affirmation:

"I am opening my mind, body, and soul and releasing all the stale energy within it."

9. Visualize a powerful light radiating from the center of your chest, slowly expanding and purging your energy field. Do this until you feel you're free of any negativity.
10. The next step is reinforcing your smudging effort with positive affirmations or prayers. You can also use sound vibrations to foster additional cleansing and balance the energy fields during smudging. Use tools that align with your vibrational frequency and force any stagnant energy to dissipate.
11. Then, start walking around slowly, and carry the smoke to each spot you want to cleanse. Once again, move the smoke around the area with your hand or a feather. Focus on places where energy could escape or hide, like windows, doorways, hallways, pieces of furniture, or plants. Use the principle from the step above for cleansing objects and tools.
12. As you watch the smoke, you might notice that it changes direction or behavior when it touches certain things. This could indicate that you should pay closer attention to these items or areas.
13. Try not to breathe in the smoke – or fill your entire space with billowing smoke. Remember, you're doing a smoke bath, not fumigating your property.
14. Seal the energetic entry points once ready to wrap up the cleansing ritual. You can do this by taking a deep breath and visualizing a powerful light radiating from the center of your chest, slowly shrinking until all your energy is fully contained within. As you do, say:

"The entryway is closed for negativity, and everything and everyone is protected."

15. Affirming the results of the smoke bath will help keep negative energies away from you so that you can remain in an open state for positive energies.

What to Do if Your Smudge Stick Goes Out

You should avoid letting the smudge stick or bundle go out during a ritual. Keep an eye on it and blow on it gently as soon as you notice it's not glowing anymore and the smoke is decreasing in intensity. It's not the end of the world if it goes out; keep your matches at hand to relight the herbs if necessary. Some herbs are harder to get burning and will die out more easily. This is normal – you'll have to pay more attention to them.

Another way to prevent smudge sticks from going out is to hold them at an angle while in use. If you have to relight the herbs, ensure the entire end of the stick remains engulfed in the flame for at least 20 seconds.

After concluding your ritual, put out the flames by pressing them in a waterproof container, abalone shell, or sink. Alternatively, you could blow on them, but some practitioners advise against this as they deem it disrespectful to the spirits. Likewise, it's not recommended to extinguish the embers with water either. Soaking the herbs could make it impossible to light them again.

If the herbs have burned down completely, or you want to banish a large amount of negativity they collected, bury them in the soil. Nature will help you dispel and neutralize those negative influences so they wouldn't come back to haunt you later.

Dealing with Stubborn Energies

In most cases, you will know that the cleansing process was successful by looking at the color of the smoke. For instance, if the smoke is thick and dark, there's a lot of energy left to clear, and when it becomes lighter, it means that the negativity is gone. However, this might not always be as easy. Some energies are so powerful and persistent that they will stubbornly cling to your objects, space, yourself, or those around you. In these instances, you should do a second (and, if needed, third) cleansing. When you do, pay attention to how the smoke moves. Does it cling to the object or parts of the space, trying to envelop it? Or is it trying to evade it? In the former case, there are still more negative energies lingering there, while in the latter case, the smoke moves away because all negative energies have been dispelled. If you're working in a room, open all the windows to let the smoke (along with the negativity) leave the space. If cleansing a non-stationary object, move it as close to the window as possible, so the tainted energy can leave immediately.

Incorporating Smudging into Your Daily Schedule

Most practitioners recommend smudging once or twice a month, depending on how frequently you encounter negative energies. However, if your practice involves regular spiritual work, you, your tools, your space, and those around you will be exposed to constant energetic interferences. To counteract their effects, incorporate regular smoke-cleaning rituals into your day-to-day life.

Wondering how to begin? It's easier than you think. Perform a quick smudging ritual every morning or evening – depending on when you work with spiritual energies. At the end of the week, do a deep cleansing of your tools, space, and, if necessary, yourself. Do additional purging tailored to specific situations. For example, if you've just hosted a large party and don't want the energies of all the attendees to taint your space, smudge them out. Smoke cleansing can also be a superb solution for clearing your aura after a disagreement with your employer or partner.

Chapter 6: Smudging Alternatives

Smokeless smudging methods can be useful when burning herbs is not practical or allowed in a particular environment. This chapter outlines various techniques and tools for energetic cleansing and purification without smoke – from sound healing through sprays and salts to visualization.

Sound Healing

Sound vibrations are a powerful tool for energy clearing and healing.[58]

Sound vibrations can be a powerful tool for energy clearing and healing. Vibration healing is a meditation or mindfulness technique which allows the participants to fully immerse themselves in higher vibrations, which carry beneficial energy. However, unlike similar methods, sound meditation can be done without setting an intention or needing outside guidance. Instead, you listen to sounds and let them soothe and heal your mind, body, and soul. This type of cleansing is particularly effective for extracting negative energy and promoting physical and emotional healing. Different sound tools like singing bowls, forks, gongs, chimes, and bells can be helpful when creating an environment for vibrational healing – also known as sound baths. Alternatively, sound baths can be concocted with calming music or pre-recorded sounds of instruments, nature, etc. The goal is to reach a deeper state of consciousness that promotes self-awareness, alleviates stress, and enables you to recharge with positive energy.

To use sound healing for cleansing, simply find a comfortable place to settle down. Close your eyes and begin to focus on your breath. As you breathe in and out, let the sound of the music or instruments permeate your senses – let it go beyond hearing. For example, you can visualize the sound waves entering your body and cleansing you from the inside out. Continue to breathe deeply and focus on the sound until you feel that you've been thoroughly cleansed.

You can also use this technique to energetically cleanse objects or spaces. For the former, place the item in a singing bowl (or near another sound source) and let the vibrations clear out the negative energy. For the latter, carry the sound source around the space. Stop a few times and let the sound rise three times in every corner or spot you stop at. Open the windows to let the negative vibes dissipate and avoid trapping them in the space.

Sprays

Smudge sprays are essential oil sprays or water-based mixtures infused with herbs or crystals conducive to purifying a space. There are different types of smudge sprays available, including:

- White sage, sweetgrass, and cedar mixture for purging negativity and replacing it with positivity.
- Essential oils of tobacco, cedar, sage, and sweetgrass for harnessing positive vibes from nature.

- Palo santo, sage, juniper, and lavender sage essences (often reinforced with rose quartz crystals) for another extra dose of positive vibes.
- Sequoia sweetgrass mixture for facilitating grounding and connecting with nature.
- White sage, hazel, cedar, and rosemary essential sprays (often enhanced with black tourmaline) for sacred rituals.

Using water alone to purify and cleanse objects, spaces, and people is a great way to sift out all the negative energies. Cleaning with water isn't just good for when you need to cleanse something or someone – but also when you want to dispel other people's tainted energies. For example, clean it before you start if you don't want anyone else's energy on a tool you prepare for a spell, ritual, or ceremony. However, for this purpose, smudge sprays work better than clear water. Similarly, you can cleanse a space or yourself with smudge sprays when you feel too much low-vibrational energy accumulated around you. If you regularly interact with different energies, do a smudge bath before going to bed or just after waking up to have a cleaner energy palette during the day.

Ingredients:

- Essential oils (use any oils mentioned above or any other one you prefer)
- Other herbal essences or herbs (you'll need to soak or cook them in hot water and let them cool down before use – in other words, make a decoction)
- Distilled water
- Pure alcohol
- Spray bottle (glass or plastic)

Instructions:

1. If you're using essential oils, pour 1.7 ounces of water into an empty glass, then add 20 drops of oils. Otherwise, use your decoctions.
2. Mix the alcohol with the water/decoction. The alcohol helps the liquid evaporate faster.
3. Pour the mixture/decoction into a diffuser or a spray bottle, then spray the room, space, or person you wish to cleanse while repeating your intention.

4. While you do, visualize white light radiating from the water, surrounding everything to restore the energetic balance.

When purging negative energies, finding the purest water source is crucial. This method uses distilled water. Nevertheless, if you have access to natural flowing springs or streams, feel free to use them. Their water comes directly from nature, so their effect will still be powerful.

Salt and Salt Baths

Salt is known for its cleansing properties and has been used to purge and clear away negative energies since ancient times. Many people still use salt to ward off negative energy. It acts as a barrier to any low vibrations that may be present. So, using salt to cleanse your space, personal items, spiritual tools - and even yourself - is a good idea. For example, sprinkling salt around your space or placing it in containers or pouches can help absorb negative energy. As an alternative, you can also use salt baths for energetic cleansing. Different types of salts have various benefits. For example, plain table salt and sea salt work best for simple cleansing rituals, black salt is a powerful energy blocker, and pink Himalayan and blue salt boost positive energy. Likewise, flaky salt is best for dispelling negative vibes and replacing them with positive ones. Do not use salt to purify silver items because it can cause rust.

Here is how to use salt for cleansing items or space:

1. Fill a small bowl with salt.
2. When cleansing your tools, place them on top or underneath the salt.
3. Leave them overnight and retrieve them the next morning. You'll have a cleansed object with refreshed energy.
4. When cleaning a room or house, mix salt with water and spray it around the space.

Here is how to cleanse your home with salt:

1. Pour a small amount of salt into a bowl and place it at your front door to stop negative energy from entering your home.
2. Remove all objects from the area you want to cleanse and dust the corners around the room, then sprinkle salt around.
3. Make sure the area remains undisturbed for a couple of days. Keep children and pets away from the salt.

The Benefits of Salt Baths

In baths, salt can be combined with any other natural cleansing agent. A salt bath can have different benefits depending on your ingredients and intention. Below are some of them.

A Balm for Your Nerves

Adding herbs to salt baths can soothe irritated nerves, restore the balance of hormones affecting the nervous system and diminish the effects of negative thoughts and emotions. All this has a wholesome influence on your overall health. Let's say you arrive home after a stressful day. You draw a salt bath, and as soon as you emerge in it, you can tune out all your worries and enjoy the soothing effects of the salt.

Lower the Effects of Stress Stimuli

Whether you feel ready to take in new sensory information or are already weighed down with what you are currently processing, sometimes, the sensory stimuli just keep coming, day after day. The environments you move in, the people you deal with, and the entertainment you consume are all packed with stimuli that affect your energy and mental state. Salt baths can help lower the energetic imprint of all those influences that threaten to disrupt your balance.

Flush Out Toxins

Soaking in the bathtub with salt water or other ingredients with antioxidant effects is far more effective than any other over-advertised detox method. It takes no time to draw water and toss in some salt and soothing herbs like rosemary, and you won't have to worry about any unwanted effects either. Spending only 20 minutes in a bathtub when you feel down will flush out all the toxins in your body, and your health will improve dramatically.

Purging Your Energy Body

Spiritual baths have a therapeutic effect on the balance of your entire energetic makeup. They replace stagnant or harmful energy with positive vibes and raise your vibrations. Salts, crystals, and essential oils are essential for cleansing your energetic body. Essential oils will also help you replace the flushed-out energy with renewed energy, especially if you spend at least 25-30 minutes soaking and relaxing in the tub.

Fostering Self-Awareness

Salt baths are a fantastic tool for creating the perfect atmosphere for contemplation. Since you're already relaxing and cleansing in your bathtub, you can also take time to do a little reflective investigation of yourself. You can ponder on your intention or think about your goals and desires. The latter works best for establishing a connection between your intuition and your higher self. You can use any exercise to gain more self-awareness and reveal your innermost desires.

Salt Water Bath to Ward off Negativity

With the following salt bath, you can relieve stress, pain, and fatigue, improve circulation, and cleanse the chakra system. It's also great for exfoliating the body, reducing skin irritation, and even healing minor injuries. While sea salt is the most effective for this purpose, you can substitute it with coarse sea salt if you don't have any available. It's a simple and effective method to ensure you'll never be affected by negative interference.

Ingredients:

- Rock or coarse sea salt
- Lavender or tea tree essential oil
- A bucket
- Lukewarm water

Instructions:

1. Make sure your bathtub is clean before you take a bath. Otherwise, residual negative energy can interfere with the bath ritual. Whether you want cleansing, protection, or healing, the number one rule is to start with a clean slate. Cleaning the bathtub and the surrounding area helps eliminate unwanted vibes from your bathroom, enabling the cleansing ritual to take full effect.

2. Pour water into a bucket until it is half full. Add the salt and a few drops of essential oils to the water. Stir until the salt has completely dissolved. While you do, establish a clear intention. Whether you want your energetic pathways cleansed, resolve negative situations in life, cleanse your body, mind, and spirit, or attract positive influences into your life – make sure you define it clearly in your mind before you even start preparing for your bath.

3. Alternatively, you can introduce music or guided meditation. Listening to meditation music or any other soothing music or even a guided meditation will help you relax and boost the benefits of spiritual cleansing and protective baths. Alternatively, you can sing

before and after the bath – there is a reason why some people love singing in the shower. It helps clear the space from negative energies that have exited your body, mind, and spirit and put them in a better mood.

4. You shouldn't focus on your phone or other electronic devices while taking a salt bath. Place the device playing the audio out of your reach.

5. Stand in your bathtub and slowly pour the salty water over your body, from head to toe. Avoid getting water into your eyes. Feel how it's cleaning you of negativity.

6. Once you've finished with the salt bath, rinse yourself off and wash your hair and body with natural soap and shampoo. The salt can dry out your skin and hair, so both will need replenishing with a good moisturizer.

7. Take your time reflecting on how you feel before and after taking the baths. Not all cleansing baths work for everyone. To establish if a particular one works for you, acknowledge what you need help with beforehand and observe the effect. Compare your results to how you felt before taking it.

8. You can repeat the bath two to three times a week, depending on how affected you are by negative energies.

When using essential oils and herbs, make sure you're familiar with their effects. Not all of them are safe for everyone, particularly if you have sensitive skin. Use only those recommended for baths. If you notice any adverse reaction from any of them, stop using them in your baths.

Visualization

Using the mind's eye to visualize a white or golden light clearing the space is another effective way to cleanse without smoke or sound. Visualization involves picturing yourself surrounded by white light or any other type of light you feel drawn to. As you envision the light surrounding you, you must focus on it cleansing your aura and washing away any negativity. Or you can also visualize the light entering your body and filling you with positivity. Alternatively, imagine the light purging objects, spaces, or another person. It all depends on your purpose. The goal is to tap into the creative parts of your brain and put aside the analytical thoughts. Using a visualization method to cleanse something or someone is a great way to get your creative juices flowing. If you're not used to visualization, it's better to practice it first for a few days before you try this cleansing ritual on any object or space.

You can do this by sitting outside in a calm atmosphere, closing your eyes, and imagining a white light descending from the sky and settling around you. Once you start feeling an energy shift, your process will be successful. The more you perform this exercise, the more effortlessly the visualized light will come to you. You can also bring other colors as well to your mind's eye.

Here's what the different colors signify:

- **White** denotes purity, peace, protection, and serenity.
- **Yellow** is associated with intellect, strength, and energy.
- **Orange** is linked to luck, confidence, and success.
- **Red** symbolizes passion, desire, power, strength, and vitality.
- **Pink** signifies peace, emotional support, compassion, and affection.
- **Purple** is attributed to wisdom, spiritual connection, and safeguarding.
- **Blue** denotes safety, protection, tranquility, and healing.
- **Green** brings luck, fortune, prosperity, abundance, balance, and healing.
- **Black** is connected to energetic shielding, binding, and warding off negativity.

You can use a color that resonates with you or when you require the properties associated with it. You can also try to visualize a combination of these colors to design and create the perfect visual. For example, you can imagine the color purple when cleansing an object and want to remove the stagnant energy. The same color will also improve your chances of connecting with the spiritual world while performing a divination technique. On the other hand, green will enable you to channel nature's energy during healing rituals. Visualize the shades that resonate best with your intuition and personal preference. Fortunately, there are no set-in-stone rules for visualizing. If your intentions are pure and you practice diligently, your efforts will pay off.

That said, here is a quick step-by-step guide for a cleansing visualization:

1. Sit in a quiet, comfortable place with no distractions. Take a deep breath, hold it briefly, and exhale. Repeat this two more times.
2. Now, close your eyes and picture a white light surrounding your body, rising all the way up to the sky. Deep down, you can sense that this light will cleanse your energy field and remove any negative or unwanted energies.
3. Visualize this light growing more intense and boisterous as it forms a grand orb around you. It moves up your body, starting at your feet and moving to your head. Then, it enters your body from your crown chakra and passes through each of the seven chakras, one by one.
4. Imagine this light flowing from your hands to the object you're holding or the space around you. See the light engulfing the item or space and absorbing all its negative energy.
5. Then, visualize this light immersing into the ground, taking the negative energy with it. Take a few deep breaths and allow yourself to relax with the knowledge that negativity won't disrupt your energy or the energy of the object or space you're cleansing anymore.
6. Once you feel thoroughly cleansed, you can open your eyes and resume your spiritual work or day-to-day activities.
7. Initially, it might take longer to channel all the negativity into the light. However, once you get the hang of this process, it'll only take a few minutes to cleanse anything you want with white or any other colored light.

Paper Cleansing

Paper cleansing is a unique smudging alternative geared toward personal purification rather than space or object cleansing.

Ingredients:
- A piece of paper
- A pen
- An incense stick (optional)
- A white candle

- Matches
- A fireproof bowl or plate (alternatively, you can use a bowl of water or a sink)

Instructions:
1. Light the candle and settle into a relaxing position.
2. Take a few deep breaths and start writing whatever comes to mind. Don't try to focus on anything – just record whatever thought or feeling comes naturally.
3. When using incense, light it and inhale its scent. Allow it to wash over your mind, body, and spirit.
4. Next, set an intention, and focus on it.
5. Bring the paper to the candle flame and burn it over the fireproof surface to avoid creating a fire hazard.
6. Visualize negativity leaving your mind, body, and spirit and getting lost in the air.
7. End your ritual with a prayer, a quick meditation, or a breathing exercise.

Chapter 7: Crafting Your Supplies

While all sorts of smudging supplies are available on the market, with so much overwhelming choice, there's nothing better than crafting your own supplies. To some people, this may seem like a waste of time and effort, but those who have truly practiced smudging, and other spiritual rituals, know the difference personalized supplies can make. You'll find all sorts of smudge sticks with different herbs and essential oils when you go to the market. Liquid smudging solutions are also abundantly present, and essential oils can be found at any local store. However, when you make your own supplies, you have the freedom to use the herbs and ingredients that are most suitable for you without having to settle for pre-made combinations. You can experiment with all sorts of herbs and choose the ones that fit your intention. You can also avoid the herbs and oils you're allergic to and those you simply don't like. There are too many pros and not enough cons to stop you from DIYing your supplies. Plus, making them is not at all difficult and can easily be mastered. This chapter will provide you with instructions to create different smudging supplies ranging from smudge sticks to smudging fans and essential oil blends.

Crafting Your Smudge Stick

The primary element you need for a smudging ritual is, of course, a smudge stick. Crafting a smudge stick is a pretty easy task, especially if you have experience with DIY crafts. Before you gather the supplies, you'll need to determine the length, thickness, and types of herbs you'll use for the smudge stick. You'll also need to get some strings to tie the bundle. The thickness and length of the smudge sticks depend entirely on you. You can make big smudge sticks with a thickness of about two inches and a length of 12 inches.

If you prefer smaller, daintier smudge sticks, the thickness can be reduced to 1 inch, and the length can be as short as three inches. People usually prefer bigger sticks when smudging a large area, as these bundles smolder slowly. On the other hand, if you just have to smudge a small room or a person, then a smaller bundle would work fine. If you're making smudge sticks for the first time, it's better to have a variety, so make both thick and thin smudge sticks just in case. The thinner ones will be best used when you're traveling or if you want to gift them to someone. The bigger ones work best for space clearing for larger spaces like a whole house or land.

Choosing something as simple as the string that will tie your smudging stick together holds significance. When the smudge stick is lit, the string will burn along with the rest of the bundle and should therefore be made from natural materials like hemp or cotton. You shouldn't use plastic strings as they release toxic chemicals when burning. The color of your string is completely your decision. Some people dye it in different colors, while others use simple undyed strings. The length needs to be much longer than your smudge sticks since it will be wrapped around the bundle several times and then tied to secure it. While the rest of the factors, like the thickness, color, and length of your smudge stick, is entirely up to you, the non-negotiable part is that your smudge stick should be secured correctly. The herbs often dry out and shrink, resulting in the sticks falling apart. To avoid this, you must tightly wrap the smudge stick with the string. Here are the supplies you'll need to craft your smudge stick:

- The herbs of your choice – you can choose from the list provided in the previous chapters but are not limited to just those herbs.
- A natural string, either colored or plain – avoid using synthetic strings.
- A pair of scissors – should be sharp.

Once you have your supplies, follow these simple steps.

1. Gather your supplies and find a flat surface to place them on. Start by separating the herbs and then arranging them in order of length and thickness. If you're using a combination of herbs, you should arrange them in a way that looks visually appealing. Make sure you don't use too many varieties in a single smudge stick, as the spiritual properties of each herb might not complement the other herbs. Instead, stick to a maximum of five herbs per smudge stick to keep a balance. If you're using rose petals, place them at the very top of your bundle to create an attractive smudge stick. Keep the shorter herbs on the outside, while the longer ones should be arranged so they are on the inside of the stick.
2. Prepare the strings by cutting them to the correct length for each smudge stick, which should be at least five times longer than the length of your herb bundle. The strings will be used to weave a pattern within your smudge sticks; therefore, they should be long enough. Keep enough strings to tie all of your smudge sticks.
3. Hold the herb bundle together with your hands, and tie a knot at the stems to secure them. Wrap the string around this knot a few times before bringing the string from the base of the stems to the tip of the bundle while holding the bundle together with one hand. Then, reverse the angle and return the string to the bundle base. Do this several times until you get a crisscross pattern, as seen on many smudge sticks.
4. When you've finished making the pattern, tie another knot to secure the wrapping. To make the smudge stick more secure, you can make some loops with the string at the base of the stems and the same loops at the top of the bundle. You can create many other patterns using your creativity or by looking them up online.
5. Once they're done, place your smudge sticks somewhere in the shade to dry out. There are two ways you can dry your smudge sticks. You can place them on a drying rack or screen with good air circulation space or hang them from a cooking rack or any other hanging place. Just be sure to keep them away from the sun so that there's little to no light where you dry them. However, air circulation is essential. They will be ready to use in about 10 days.

How to Make a Smudging Fan

Next on your list of smudging supplies is the smudging fan, and contrary to what you may think, making smudging fans isn't a difficult process either. You only need creativity, feathers, and decorative elements to create an elaborative smudging fan. When it comes to making them, the sky is your creative limit. Some common items used to make smudging fans include beads, crystals, shells, twigs, cords, and leather pouches. In fact, you can use any piece of nature that speaks to you and can be attached to the fan, whether it's some twigs, pinecones, or even leaves. People have made ocean-themed fans with beautiful shells and dried sea vegetation adorning the surface. Forest themes are also common, with antlers, twigs, and small pinecones used to decorate the fans.

You can also decorate your fan with bright-colored feathers, tassels, and crystals. You can even use just one feather adorned with a crystal as your smudging fan. Using a smudging fan during the ritual significantly impacts the process, as compared to using just your hand to wave the smoke around. It brings light energy to the smoke and ensures that the smudging energy gets to every part of the room. You can use real bird feathers collected from the wild or artificial feathers to make your fan. According to ancient traditions, smudging fans used to be made from the whole wing of an eagle, so the concept of a smudging fan is to replicate a bird's wing. Here are the supplies you'll need for your fan:

- Variety of feathers (collected from walks in nature or purchased from a craft store)
- Small and sturdy branch, driftwood, or a piece of wood (2 to 5 inches long)
- Glue gun
- Cord made from leather or another preferred material

Decorative items like crystals, small beads, personal talismans, or other appealing items When you have all your supplies ready, follow these simple steps:

1. Gather the materials on a large, flat surface, ideally a kitchen counter or a craft table. You'll be using a glue gun to attach the decorations, so be mindful of protecting the surface from the hot glue.

2. Divide the materials into four portions, place the feathers on one side, the decoration items on another, and the branch to be used as the base and glue gun in the center.
3. First, you need to arrange the feathers for the fan. Start by separating the feathers based on size and color. It's suggested that you use the same color feathers for the fan, but you can also be creative.
4. Place the larger feathers at the back and the smaller ones up front. The arrangement should resemble a bird's wing. Ensure all the feathers are facing the same direction.
5. After you've arranged the feathers, pick up the branch, and work out which side of the stick will be used as the front side of the fan. Then, apply glue to the base and attach the feathers, one at a time.
6. Keep attaching the feathers side by side and then on top of one another until the fan has enough wings.
7. Now, take the leather cord, and wrap it around the branch, either completely or partially. This is up to you. Use glue to firmly attach the leather to the wood.
8. Finally, select the decorations you want to use, and visualize the design you want to create. Before gluing the items onto the fan, first place them in their planned positions, and see if the fan looks good. Then, you can glue each item onto the feathers.

Your smudging fan is ready! Place this on your altar, along with the rest of the smudging supplies. If you're traveling and need to carry your smudging fan with you, pack it properly beforehand, either with bubble wrap or plastic sheets.

Liquid Smudging

Liquid smudging is one of the easiest ways to rid your space of negative energy and replenish the positive essence in your surroundings. Many of you may have decided to opt for liquid smudging – as it doesn't require much effort or require you to deal with smoke. The best part? You can make your own liquid smudging blend by choosing between a selection of essential oils. Or, you can follow the recipe below to make a liquid smudge blend of lavender, white sage, and several other powerful herbs.

Here are the supplies you will need:
- 15 drops of cedar essential oil
- 4-ounce bottle
- 15 drops of lavender essential oil
- 4 ounces of pure water

25 drops of white sage essential oil Once you've gathered your materials, the rest of the steps are pretty simple:

1. Wash and dry your bottle to ensure there are no impurities in the blend.
2. Add the essential oils to the water and mix thoroughly.
3. Pour this solution into the 4-ounce bottle, and screw it closed.

Your liquid smudging blend is ready for use! Always shake the bottle before every application. To experiment with the recipe, you can change the base oil, which is white sage essential oil. It's best to avoid adding too many different essential oils into the solution if you do not want to get rid of the main tone of the blend. Some other essential oils that go well with white sage include:

- Frankincense
- Lemon oil
- Wild orange
- Lime
- Geranium
- Cedarwood
- Sandalwood

If you want to make a more powerful blend, you can add a bit of unprocessed sea salt to the mixture, as it is said to amplify the effect of space cleansing. Alternatively, you can add a small crystal to the liquid smudging bottle. To do this, you must first charge the crystal by letting it sit in a bowl of water under direct sunlight for three days. Then, you can use this solar-charged crystal – and even the water in your smudging blend. This will add the fiery energy of the sun to your blend and make it even more effective in dispelling the negative energies in your spaces.

Of course, you must ensure the crystal is small enough to fit inside the tiny bottle. If it doesn't, you can still use the crystal-charged water for the blend. This is because water has memory and can carry vibrations inside its medium. So, when you let it charge by using the crystal's energy for several days, it will contain the positive energies carried by the crystal. Another alternative is to use Agua de Floride, which is basically a blend of different floral essences and scents in an alcohol base.

This blend is quite popular for creating different essential oil blends or other holistic solutions. Many shamans use it to cleanse and purify their energy and to protect and ground their auras. In fact, you can use it without any other additions to clear your space of negative essences by spraying it into the air. This is especially helpful when you're on the move, in a new space, or simply cannot prepare for a full-fledged smudging ritual.

Essential Oil Blends

In addition to liquid smudging, you can create some essential oil blends for your aromatherapy diffuser. The only difference between the two is the addition of water, followed by the spraying process. When using a diffuser, there isn't much to worry about; just put these essential oil blends into the diffuser and let it do its job!

You'll need only two supplies to create your essential oil blends; a small bottle (preferably made with dark-colored glass) and your selection of essential oils. Mix the essential oils and pour them into the glass bottle to make the blend. You'll need to store these blends away from heat and sunlight, as that can weaken their potency. Below are some easy recipes of essential oil blends, perfect for promoting healing energy and protecting your space from negative energy:

Heavy clearing essential oil blend:

This blend can be used to clear extremely toxic and negative energies from your space and your aura. If this feels a bit too intense, you can try the other recipes first. You can also choose not to use all of the essential oils mentioned in the recipe and stick with just two or three of the options shown. Pour the essential oil blends into the diffuser bowl and enjoy the fragrance:

- 15 drops – lemon essential oil
- 5 drops – pine or juniper essential oil
- 10 drops – peppermint essential oil
- 5 drops – eucalyptus essential oil

- 20 drops - lavender essential oil
- 20 drops - rosemary essential oil
- 5 drops - rose geranium essential oil (optional)

Cleansing and attracting good energy blend:

This harmonious fusion of essential oils can work wonders in purifying your surroundings while effortlessly attracting positive energy. This blend can create an inviting and revitalizing atmosphere where freshness and positivity thrive.

- 25 drops - lemon essential oil
- 15 drops - grapefruit essential oil
- 10 drops - peppermint essential oil (optional)
- 30 drops - tangerine essential oil
- 15 drops - lavender essential oil

If the process of counting drops for your blend makes you anxious, rest assured that it's common to err on the side of adding more rather than less. There's no need to worry because you can hardly go wrong with it. So, take a deep breath, relax, and let the diffuser do its magic. If you feel the scent isn't strong enough, simply pause the diffuser and add a couple more drops of essential oil. It's as simple as that!

When crafting your own supplies for smudging, there's something truly special about doing it yourself. Not only does it let you add a personal touch and infuse your intentions with your personality, but it also brings a whole different energy compared to store-bought goods. Remember to give them the respect they deserve when storing your smudging supplies. Find a cozy spot on your altar or another sacred space to keep them. Treating them with care keeps their energy intact and ensures they're ready to bring you magic when needed. When you take the time to craft your own supplies for smudging and store them respectfully, you're creating a special bond with the tools of your spiritual practice.

Chapter 8: Psychic Protection Methods

Your energy is constantly under attack because people around you can send you negative vibes, consciously or subconsciously."

You may not be aware of it, but your energy is constantly under attack. People around you can send you negative vibes, consciously or subconsciously. Some may do this to harm you or your loved ones mentally, physically, or spiritually. Even those closest to you can be secretly harboring feelings of anger, jealousy, or resentment toward you.

This negative energy can disturb your peace of mind and prevent blessings from coming your way. You shouldn't leave yourself vulnerable to psychic attacks. You can use various techniques with smudging to shield you from negativity and all the people who want to cause you harm.

This chapter will explain how to identify psychic attacks and provide techniques to defend yourself in these situations.

Signs You Are Under Psychic Attacks

Some physical and mental afflictions aren't medical. If you get checked up, do all the necessary tests, and find nothing is wrong, you may be under psychic attacks. Identifying the symptoms of these attacks will give you an idea of what you are dealing with so you can take precautions to protect yourself.

Bad Luck

If you are a victim of psychic attacks, you will feel like you are cursed or experiencing a series of bad luck. Negative energy and entities affect your aura and block your chakras, attracting negative experiences and preventing good fortune from entering your life. No matter what you do, nothing goes your way. It can sometimes feel like you are the unluckiest person on the planet. Your life will be chaotic. You will constantly fight with your loved ones, start acting differently, and won't be able to recognize yourself.

Nightmares

When you are asleep, you are in your most vulnerable state, and your auric field can be susceptible to negative energy. Nightmares, sleep paralysis, or night terrors are often signs of psychic attacks. Bad dreams can be so vivid that they terrify you. The situation can be so severe that you will dread going to sleep, making you feel exhausted the next day.

Exhaustion

Negative energy drains you mentally, physically, and emotionally making you constantly exhausted. You will lose your spark and will have no desire to chase your goals. You won't even have the energy to get out of bed. In severe cases, this can lead to isolation and depression.

Negative Thoughts

Naturally, negative energy will lead to negative thoughts. These thoughts can be so intrusive, resulting in unexplainable phobias and fears. Negative energy will manipulate your thoughts and emotions and create false narratives to distort your reality.

Constant Fear

Negative energy is like a hunter that wants to catch you at your most vulnerable moment. Therefore, it will play on your fears and even exaggerate them in your mind to make you easy prey.

Being Watched

If you constantly feel that someone is watching you to the point that it makes you feel paranoid, you are under psychic attacks.

Gifts

Strangely, you can experience odd emotional, mental, or physical symptoms after receiving a gift from someone.

Accidents

Psychic attacks can make you accident-prone. People experience small accidents occasionally, like falling in the bathroom, dropping and breaking a glass of water, or pouring coffee over themselves. However, if you experience these accidents more than usual and you begin to feel something isn't right, you could be influenced by psychic attacks.

Losing Stuff

Who doesn't lose their stuff? You have probably lost more white socks than you can count. However, if you have been misplacing most of your items, like your cellphone or laptop, lately, negative energy may have affected you.

Indecisiveness

Have you been struggling with making decisions lately? Psychic attacks can make it hard for you to tap into your intuition to take action or make the necessary decisions.

Pain and Illness

If you don't suffer from any medical problems yet get sick or experience sharp pain, you could suffer from psychic attacks.

Heaviness

Negative emotions are a hard burden to carry. Psychic attacks can make you feel like you are carrying the weight of the world on your shoulders.

There is no denying that symptoms of psychic attacks can be both frustrating and scary. Luckily, there are effective techniques that you can practice with smudging to shield yourself from these attacks once and for all.

Grounding

Grounding, also called earthing, is a process where you connect your body with the Earth to feel rooted to Mother Nature and bring balance and stability to your body and life. It is also a meditation technique that can make you mindful, aware of your surroundings, and focused on the here and now so you won't be preoccupied with negative thoughts. Grounding is an effective remedy against many symptoms of psychic attacks like anxiety, stress, fear, forgetfulness, and feeling overwhelmed. These techniques also connect you with your body and your five senses so you focus within and quieten the negative thoughts.

Grounding exercises give you control over your energy to unblock your chakras and allow positive energy to flow through you and heal your body, mind, and spirit. Grounding will reverse the effect of psychic attacks making you more secure, confident, balanced, and energetic, and improve your sleep.

Since you interact with different people daily, you can never know where the next attack is coming from. You need to protect yourself from this potentially negative experience. Several grounding techniques can act as shields so you can live your day-to-day life without worrying about the negative energy of others.

Grounding Technique

Instructions:

1. Find a quiet place outdoors, like in your garden or backyard, or you can go to the park or anywhere in a natural environment.
2. Stand barefoot with both feet firmly touching the ground.
3. Breathe in and out slowly and deeply for a couple of minutes.
4. Close your eyes and visualize roots coming from your feet and reaching the ground. They extend so far right into the earth's core.
5. Now, release the negative energy from your mind and body through the roots and into the earth.

Grounding Protection Technique
Instructions:
1. Sit or stand in a quiet place away from distractions.
2. Take a few deep and slow breaths.
3. Close your eyes and imagine a big protective ball of white light surrounding you, covering your whole body as if embracing you to keep you safe from harm.
4. Fill the ball with positive energy, light, joy, love, and other warm emotions.
5. Next, imagine dark entities, negative emotions, and thoughts as arrows attacking you from all directions.
6. If this image makes you tense, keep your breathing steady and calm yourself.
7. Now, imagine the arrows bouncing off the white ball. You feel safe and protected. Nothing in this world can ever harm you.

The 5, 4, 3, 2, and 1 Technique
This is a simple technique where you list different objects in your environment that you can experience with your five senses, starting from five to one.

Instructions:
1. Sit in a comfortable position and look around you.
2. In your head, list in your head five objects you can see.
3. Four objects you can hear.
4. Three objects you can feel or touch.
5. Two objects you can smell.
6. One thing you can taste.

Breathing Technique
Instructions:
1. Breathe in deeply while counting to four.
2. Hold your breath for seven seconds.
3. Breathe out slowly while counting to eight.

Feel your body moving with every breath, and pay attention to how it feels. Be present in the moment and notice how your body changes when you inhale, hold your breath, and exhale.

Shielding

Shielding is a technique that protects you from intrusive and negative energy. You place an invisible energy shield around you to keep you safe and prevent psychic attacks from getting to you. You must practice shielding techniques whenever you feel tired, drained, and emotionally imbalanced.

The idea of shielding can seem otherworldly, and you may think you need to be a psychic or have special abilities to protect yourself. However, this process is simple, and anyone can practice it. You are made of energy, so think of this shield as an extension of yourself. It is a part of you that always surrounds you while keeping you safe.

Similar to setting boundaries with people, a shield screens all types of energy you deal with daily and filters the bad energy out, only letting positive and warm energy in. So, no one can invade your energetic field without your permission.

There are various shielding techniques that you can easily practice, and they are all equally effective.

Shielding Visualization

Instructions:

1. Find a quiet spot and sit in a comfortable position.
2. Take slow and deep breaths, and imagine you are releasing the tension and stress in your body with every breath.
3. Keep breathing until you feel relaxed.
4. Close your eyes and think about creating a shield around you to protect your energy.
5. The shield will be made of warm and blue light since the color symbolizes protection.
6. Now, set an intention. You can say something like, *"I intend to create a shield made of wisdom, light, and divine love to keep me safe from negative entities and intrusive energy."*
7. Next, visualize multiple mirrors facing outward, surrounding you from all sides, above and under you. Any negative energy that tries to come near you will be reflected back by the mirrors.
8. You have now created an energy shield that is sealed from all directions keeping you safe at all times and preventing any

negativity from coming near you.

9. Now, set another intention that you will only allow positive energy and emotions to enter through the shield. You can say something like, *"I set an intention for only joy, love, and positive emotions and thoughts to pass through my shield."*
10. Visualize a rose quartz crystal radiating warm and pink light. The light is all around you, embracing you and making you feel loved and protected.
11. Now, your energy shield is complete. Sit for a couple of minutes while thinking of your intention. Enjoy the feeling of protection.
12. Memorize how the shield feels and think of this feeling whenever you are around negative people.

Jaguar Meditation

In different cultures, the jaguar is a symbol of protection.

Instructions:

1. Sit in a comfortable position in a quiet space.
2. For this technique to work, you should be calm and relaxed. You can place a few drops of essential oil in a diffuser and place it where you will practice this technique to keep you calm and reduce stress. You can also practice the 5, 4, 3, 2, and 1 breathing exercise.
3. Once you feel calm, close your eyes and call on the jaguar's power to surround you with its protection.
4. Prepare yourself to accept the healing and protective love of the animal and to feel it with every part of your being.
5. Visualize the jaguar entering your energy field, protecting you, and keeping your energy safe from negative entities and unwanted energy.
6. Keep visualizing the jaguar and focus on it. Notice the way it moves with power, confidence, and grace.
7. The jaguar runs around you in circles, creating a protective shield and making you feel at peace because you know nothing can penetrate this shield.
8. End the meditation by giving thanks to the jaguar for its protection.

Energy Work

Energy work, also known as energy healing, is a practice that involves using Chi or energy life force to unblock your chakras and bring harmony, balance, and healing energy into your life. Energy work includes various techniques like tapping, massage, breathing exercises, healing crystals, reflexology, acupuncture, light therapy, reiki, and smudging. You can practice Some of these techniques while others, like acupuncture and reiki, require a professional.

Breathwork

Instructions:

1. Sit in a comfortable position and place your right hand over your belly.
2. Feel your belly expand as you inhale and feel the air release from your belly, emptying it as you exhale.
3. Put your left hand over your ribs and take a long deep breath. Feel your ribs expand while softening your belly.
4. Move your left hand to your upper chest. Breathe in, feeling your chest broadening, your ribs expanding, and your belly softening.
5. Breathe out and let out all the negativity.
6. Repeat these steps three to 10 times before any smudging ritual.

Meditation with Crystals

Instructions:

1. Choose the right crystals for you (the next chapter will explain this process in detail).
2. Set an intention. Say something like, *"I intend to use this meditation to release negative energy and protect myself from psychic attacks."*
3. Play relaxing music to keep you calm.
4. Sit in a comfortable position and hold one crystal in your right hand and place the others around you. You can lie down if you prefer and place the crystals over your body.
5. Take slow and deep breaths.

6. Close your eyes and imagine the crystals radiating warm and protective light surrounding you and keeping you safe.
7. Sit with this feeling until you feel protected.

Spirit Guides

Spirit guides are energy entities that provide guidance and support. Every person has one, and if you haven't felt it, they just haven't connected with you yet. They are always nearby helping you even when you don't ask for it. They can send you messages through dreams, symbols, or strange situations that you may brush off as coincidences. If you connect with your spirit guide, you will be able to decipher the messages they send you.

Your spirit guide can be an angel, animal, bird, or deceased ancestor. It is powerful and can protect you against all types of psychic attacks. Connecting with them will make it easier to ask for their help whenever you need protection.

Connecting with Your Spirit Guide
Instructions:
1. Create a sacred space like building an altar, or simply choose an undisturbed room and cleanse it.
2. Set an intention to practice this technique to communicate with your spirit guide.
3. Close your eyes and ask your spirit guide to join you.
4. Take a few deep breaths and clear your mind. Only focus on your spirit guide.
5. Say, "*Welcome, my spirit guide; please give me a sign you are here.*"
6. You will hear a voice, see an image, smell a scent, or get a feeling when they are here. Keep an open mind, and you will pick up on something. This may not happen immediately, and you may need to repeat this technique a few times until you can successfully communicate with them.
7. Once you notice their presence, ask for their help to protect you against psychic attacks while performing a smudging ritual.
8. You can see an image of white light surrounding you and protecting you or simply feel protected. Your guide will show

you in some way that they are keeping you safe.

9. When you feel protected, thank your spirit guide for their assistance and slowly open your eyes.

Smudging

You can practice smudging techniques to protect yourself against psychic attack symptoms.

Instructions:

1. Burn sage in a metallic bowl.
2. Let it burn until it releases thick smoke.
3. Hold the sage and cleanse yourself, starting with your head and moving down to every part of your body.
4. Imagine the negative energy separating from you and the smoke protecting you.
5. Leave the sage to finish burning.

Common Challenges When Smudging

Some common challenges and obstacles can crop up when practicing smudging for psychic protection. You can't protect yourself unless you silence these thoughts and believe in the power of this ritual.

Skepticism from Others

Some of your family members or friends may think it's strange that you use smoke to protect yourself from psychic attacks. They can either mock you or be skeptical. Either way, you shouldn't care what others think. Love and respect them but understand that each person has their own beliefs. They probably believe in things you don't agree with, but you respect those differences, and they should also.

However, if their skepticism bothers you, you can show them the history of smudging and how it has been an effective method for psychic protection for centuries. You can also show them all the scientific research proving smoke has strong healing properties.

Whether they start to believe in smudging or not, remember you have nothing to prove to anyone.

Difficulties with Visualization

Visualization is a big part of psychic protection methods. However, this technique doesn't come easily to everyone. A few simple tips can ignite your imagination so you can create images in your mind.

- If you struggle with visualizing a specific image, try to conjure an event from your past. Think of the sounds, smells, and feelings associated with it, and keep focusing on them until you see an image.
- Sometimes, a smell can easily bring an image to mind. For instance, the smell of your grandmother's cooking will make you picture her and her house. The sound of a school bell can conjure up images of your childhood friends.
- Use songs, images, scents, food, and even objects you can touch – something that reminds you of a person or an event in your life. Whenever an image appears in your head, press on your thumb. In time, this can become an anchor, something you use to get you in the zone to visualize.

Self-Doubt

- You may not believe in yourself or your abilities. You think you don't have it in you to protect yourself from psychic attacks. Believing in yourself comes from within; get to the bottom of the self-doubt issue to relinquish it.
- Try journaling. Think of why you are doubting yourself, and write down all thoughts and feelings that you experience. The more you write, the easier you will get to the source of your doubts.
- When you discover the source, ask yourself more questions, like are your doubts reasonable or if you can control the thoughts that hold you back.
- Self-doubt stems from negative thoughts. By now, you understand that these thoughts aren't based on anything real. In the case of psychic attacks, the negative thoughts you experience aren't yours. They are transferred to you from someone else. You can use all the information you have on negative thoughts to rid yourself of them. Once these thoughts go away, so will your self-doubt.

Psychic attacks are serious and can impact every aspect of your life. However, smudging and all the techniques in this chapter can protect you and keep you safe at all times.

Chapter 9: Crystals and Smudging

Crystals are beautiful, colorful, and powerful stones. They come from stardust, lava, minerals, and other natural resources. Crystals contain energy, and since every human being is made from energy, you can exchange your negative vibes with the crystals' positive energy.

The wisdom and knowledge of crystals often feel spiritual rather than earthly. Every crystal has its own unique properties and radiates vibes matching its environment. They can cleanse, heal, and purify your spirit, body, and physical space. Therefore, you can use them in a smudging ritual for their cleansing and healing properties.

Crystals Used in Smudging

Although there are over four thousand crystals in the world, each has its own functions and uses. The first part of the chapter will cover the most common crystals used in smudging and their spiritual properties.

Clear Quartz

Clear quartz crystal.[55]

The clear quartz crystal is a transparent stone that provides healing, connects with your seven chakras, and amplifies power by significantly increasing the energy you pour into it and strengthening the vibrations of other crystals as well. It also cleanses your energy and surroundings. It often comes from frozen waters, and it resembles pieces of ice and radiates cooling energy. Since ancient times, this stone has been associated with myth, mysticism, and magic.

This crystal provides spiritual growth by pushing you to look within and discover who you truly are. It also unblocks the chakras, allowing energy to follow easily in your body and cleanse your aura. The clear quartz is associated with the crown chakra located over the top of your head. This chakra connects you with the Divine, higher planes of existence, and all the endless possibilities in the universe. It can balance, store, or release energy and bring you wisdom and awareness.

Clear quartz can improve your mental clarity, stabilize your emotions, and bring focus to whatever you desire. You can also use it for meditation and during manifestation rituals. This crystal has protective properties and can enhance your psychic powers. It has the unique ability to open your eyes to your truth and the truth of the people in your life so you can understand yourself better and see every situation from a different and fresh perspective. It can also bring harmony to your personal life and environment and mental and emotional clarity as well.

For this reason, it is often referred to as "The Universal Crystal" since it can be used in many aspects, like channeling, protection, meditation, and manifestation, and it is one of the most powerful and effective healing stones.

Amethyst

Amethyst crystal.[56]

Amethyst is a beautiful purple crystal that radiates wisdom, calmness, and spiritual healing. It acts as a bridge that connects the physical world with the spiritual world, the Divine, and provides spiritual awakening. For centuries, this stone has been associated with spirituality, the crown chakra, and the third eye.

"Amethyst" is derived from the Greek word "*Amethystos*," meaning "non-intoxicated" because the ancient Greeks used to wear it for protection against the effect of intoxication. The crystal has always been connected with magic and myth. In ancient Greek and Roman mythology, it is believed that amethyst got its color from the tears of the god of wine.

The legend says that Amethyst was a young virgin girl who was treated badly by Dionysus/Bacchus (gods of wine in Greek and Roman mythology, respectively) whenever he was drunk. She couldn't take it anymore and begged Diana/Artemis (goddesses of hunting and wild animals in Roman and Greek mythology) to help make her pain stop.

So, the goddess turned her into a white stone. When the god of wine found out what had happened, he cried over the crystal until it turned purple. Thanks to this legend, amethyst has long since been associated with mental clarity and contemplation.

Everyone has intuition. They just don't know how to use it. The amethyst crystal unblocks your third eye and brings your sixth sense to life. It also awakens your intuition and invites wisdom and imagination into your life. The crystal is also connected to the crown chakra that opens you up to receive messages from the divine and the universe. It protects you against negative energy, bad emotions, and black magic.

Amethyst has strong spiritual vibes that increase your awareness. It can bring you closer to your guardian angel and spiritual guides. It gives you knowledge and shows you that you are one with the universe. The stone can fill your heart with Divine love and spiritual wisdom and reminds you that you aren't alone in the world. It improves your psychic abilities and facilitates visions and out-of-body experiences, and alters your energy to raise its frequency.

Black Tourmaline

Black tourmaline.[87]

Black tourmaline is one of the strongest crystals to use against negative energy and bad emotions. Although tourmaline comes in different colors, none is as powerful as the black one. The crystal is associated with the Muladhara chakra, the first of the chakras that makes you feel grounded and safe in your environment. The stone protects you against psychic attacks and energy vampires (negative people who drain your energy, leaving you feeling tired) and raises your vibrations. Black tourmaline purifies your body and surroundings from negative energy and dark entities. It elevates your consciousness and puts you on the path of enlightenment. It teaches you how to live a life in the service of others so you can make a difference in the world.

Ancient cultures used black tourmaline for its protective properties since it soaks up all negativity and acts as a shield against harmful energy.

Don't let its dark color fool you. Black tourmaline can also bring light and clarity to your environment. When life gets tough, and you feel stuck in your situation, this crystal will radiate light and positive energy, bring the love of the universe into your heart, and elevate your spiritual consciousness. It connects you to higher forces, balances your chakras, and encourages spiritual healing. Black tourmaline wands have unique properties as they can channel powerful energy that transcends the physical world to provide healing. They can also release negative energy from your aura to allow positivity to flow through your being.

You can use black tourmaline in spiritual meditation as it can safely take you to the spiritual world. If you dream of this crystal, it's a warning against danger.

Selenite

Selenite crystal.^a

This pearly white crystal owes its name to Selene, the Greek goddess of the moon. This makes it one of the most spiritual stones. If you look at it, you will sense a calmness washing over you. Its soothing qualities come from its pale white color that looks and feels otherworldly. In ancient Greece, Selenite was favored by the goddesses because it brings spiritual healing, harmony, and protection to your mind, body, and physical space.

The crystal can increase your vibrations so you can receive and interpret meaningful messages from the universe. It can unblock your seven chakras to facilitate energy flow, protect you against negative energy and entities, and bring purity and peace to your heart and mind.

Although selenite can provide mental, physical, and emotional healing, its most powerful attributes are in the spiritual and metaphysical realms. It can cleanse your aura and connect you with your spirit guide and highest self. Working with this stone can enhance your psychic abilities, open you up to discover all levels of your consciousness, access your past lives so you can heal from traumatic events, connect you to the spirit and angel world, and show you the path to the Divine.

The stone can bring positivity into your life and reminds you that you are a child of God and a part of the universe who deserves to be happy. It pushes you forward to become the best version of yourself. It clears your vision so you can discover your passion and goals. It eliminates negative thoughts leading you to talk about yourself and your goals using positive and powerful statements. You can use this crystal in smudging, scrying, meditation, and manifestation.

Rose Quartz

Rose Quartz crystal.[89]

Rose quartz belongs to the same family as clear quartz. It radiates positive and tender emotions and has become a symbol of love for centuries. Its healing properties can bring harmony into your life; most people love keeping it near them. It is associated with the throat chakra and the heart chakra. It can heal conflict and trauma in all types of relationships, whether romantic or not.

This crystal can unblock your heart chakra to open it up to love, joy, and other positive emotions. It can bring balance to your life, connect you to the world around you and the people in your life, bring you comfort, and show you all the possibilities in life. Rose quartz is linked to the female energy of the goddesses, attracts peace and compassion to your aura, and empowers your spirit. Its healing properties can calm your soul, show you your true potential, and comfort your broken heart. It releases negative emotions like hatred, resentment, fear, and anger to purify your soul and end your pain.

The stone connects your heart to the Earth and the universe, giving you the courage to love and express your emotions without fear. After experiencing the healing properties of rose quartz, you will feel like a new person. You will be kinder, more hopeful, and your faith in yourself and the world will be restored. The stone will remind you that the secret to happiness is to love the people in your life unconditionally without waiting for anything in return, and the universe will send the same kind of love your way. You will learn that all of God's creation should be cherished and treated with respect.

Rose quartz has a motherly and nurturing presence, which you can use for support during harsh times. Its warm energy can make you feel loved, protected, and content and make you believe that anything is possible. It pushes you to ask yourself tough questions to show you that the answers are often simpler than you think.

Citrine

Citrine crystal.[60]

Citrine is another crystal that belongs to the quartz family. This yellow stone can bring light and sunshine into your life and remind you that brighter days are ahead of you. It is linked to the solar plexus chakra and the sacral chakra. It keeps you grounded and brings balance and stability into your life. The crystal can unblock the solar plexus chakra to empower you and make you feel that you can handle anything life throws your way.

This crystal opens up your sacral chakra and brings intimacy, passion, and creativity into your life. It can also protect you against negative energy, empower your spirit, and invite positivity into your heart. You will be able to smile through the pain because you know things will always get better.

Suppose you are sensitive or easily affected by negative energies and entities. In that case, citrine can act as a shield to protect you from harmful influences. It is an abundance crystal that you can use to manifest success, prosperity, wealth, and a variety of wonderful things. During family conflicts, citrine can calm you down so you can think clearly and prevent the situation from escalating.

It also awakens your psychic abilities to understand the information and signs the universe sends to you. For some people, it can guide them to astral projects. It can also align and cleanse your aura, bring light and clarity to it, and provide mental and emotional healing.

The stone enhances your connection with your higher self and the Divine. People commonly use it during rituals and meditation to keep them grounded and invite enlightenment and awareness.

Obsidian

Obsidian.[61]

Obsidian is a powerful dark crystal that protects you against negative energy. Although it is a black stone, it shows you that you can see through the darkness to discover the truth. Its clear surface resembles a mirror reflecting a vision of the future. Some believe they can use its clear surface to awaken their higher consciousness.

The crystal is linked to the root chakra that keeps you grounded even if your world is turning upside down. Obsidian can unblock your root chakra, allowing for smooth energy flow, making you feel safe and strong, and protecting you against psychic attacks. Ancient cultures used this stone to awaken the third eye chakra and to visit the spiritual world.

Each person has a dark side that they aren't usually aware of. Obsidian reveals this side to you to show you a different side of your personality. It uncovers your strengths, weaknesses, capabilities, and even parts of yourself that you have forgotten. The crystal gives your soul a purpose, enhances spiritual growth, and pushes you to explore the mysteries of the universe.

The stones align your spirit with your mind and body, release negative energy, and invite harmony and peace into your life.

Methods of Incorporating Crystals into a Smudging Practice

This part of the chapter will focus on the different ways you can use crystals in your smudging rituals.

Placing Crystals around the Space

Before smudging, placing crystals around the space amplifies the energy and supports the cleansing process. Good crystals for this purpose include clear quartz, amethyst, black tourmaline, and selenite.

You can also create a crystal grid by arranging the stones into a sacred geometric position to strengthen their energy. There are various grids you can find online, or you can use grid cloths.

Crystal Wand

Use a crystal wand to direct the smoke from the smudge stick. Choose one that fits your intentions or needs (a clear quartz wand for amplifying energy or a rose quartz wand for love and healing). You can choose a crystal wand by holding it in your hand. If you connect with it immediately, it is the right stone for you. If you shop online, you can use the information here to guide you.

Ask yourself why you are performing this ritual. Do you want to cleanse your surroundings? Do you want to protect yourself against negative energy? Or do you want to amplify the energy of an object? Your answers will determine which crystal to use.

Build a Crystal Altar

Build an altar and add one or more crystals to it. You can perform smudging rituals at the altar to harness the stones' energy.

Holding Crystals

Holding crystals while smudging infuses them with cleansing energy and helps them focus on your intentions.

To set your intention, follow these simple instructions:
1. Hold the stone with your dominant hand.
2. Close your eyes and clear your mind.
3. Take a few deep and slow breaths until you feel grounded.
4. Imagine yourself standing in nature, taking in the beautiful scenery and feeling calm and relaxed.
5. Imagine there is a large version of the crystal right before you.
6. Step inside the crystal to explore it. Visualize every part of the inside of the crystal, like its scent, look, sound, and the feeling you experience at this moment. Everything should look and feel real.
7. Now focus on your intention and fill the inside of the crystal with people, colors, symbols, objects, etc., associated with your goal and what you hope to achieve from this ritual.
8. After adding the final touches, sit, and take in your surroundings.
9. When you feel comfortable, repeat your intention out loud in real life and in the visualization.
10. Imagine yourself carving or writing every word of your intention on the inside walls of your crystal.
11. Sit in your crystal for a while. Walk around and study every part of it. Spread positive every all around.
12. You can now use it in your ritual.

Charging/Programming Crystals with Smoke

After smudging, hold crystals in the smoke to cleanse and charge them. This can help to reset their energy and enhance their healing properties. Remember, there is negative energy all around you. During the ritual, your crystals can absorb this energy, affecting your surroundings and ruining your next ritual. Cleansing the crystals will release all the bad energy and entities, charging your crystal with loving and positive vibes.

Instructions:
1. Pass your crystal over the smoke for a couple of minutes.
2. Set an intention to charge your crystal with positive energy and release negative energy.

Crystals are extremely powerful and can amplify the energy and healing properties during any smudging rituals. Before choosing a stone, study its spiritual and healing properties to find the one that fits your needs. When buying a crystal, don't just take the first one you see. Let the right one call out to you. Keep an open mind, and let your heart guide you. You will often establish a connection with your crystal right away. Once you choose, cleanse it using smoke and infuse it with your intention and positive energy. In a short time, you will begin to notice the powerful impact of these enchanting stones on your ritual.

Chapter 10: Healing with Smudging

Throughout the book, you will have encountered several instances showing the power of healing through smudging. And suppose you have already tried some of the techniques before reaching this point. In that case, you may have experienced its restorative properties for yourself. Indeed, one of the lesser-known secrets of smudging is its capacity to heal numerous ailments, not just physical diseases but spiritual and emotional maladies as well.

Healing Physical Diseases

Studies have shown that sage, the herb most commonly used for smudging, has antibacterial and antimicrobial properties. In its natural environment, sage is known to repel some of the most harmful insects as well. Did you know that the herb is an antioxidant that can eliminate over 90% of bacteria in a room?

Here's another interesting fact: sage is called *salvia* in Latin, and *salvia*'s linguistic roots can be traced to the word *heal* (Harry Potter fans might know the spell *salvio hexia*, used to repel physically harmful hexes). Burning sage can boost your immunity and protect you from various diseases.

The other herbs used in smudging rituals also contain several physical healing properties.

- **Cedar**

  Like sage, cedar also repels insects. If you inhale the cedar smoke generated by smudging, it will open up your air pipes, allowing you to breathe more freely while helping you take care of any existing respiratory diseases. And are you often prone to arthritis? Cedar smudging may help ease the pain and reduce the inflammation in your joints.

- **Palo Santo**

  The smoke from palo santo smudging may cure several respiratory ailments like asthma. Its wood oil may be used to cure arthritis, and it may even improve your skin health. Research suggests that the d-limonene compound found in palo santo wood may help protect you from cancer.

- **Sweetgrass**

  The smoke from burning sweetgrass is known to heal the common cold. If you make tea out of this plant, it may even cure your incessant coughs and fever. The oil from sweetgrass may heal your wounds by its virtue of repelling bacteria.

- **Lavender**

  Over the years, lavender smoke has been used to relieve headaches and migraines. It is possible to reduce joint inflammation and alleviate muscle aches with the plant. Its antibacterial properties may help cure eczema. Additionally, lavender smudging improves both blood and air circulation in your body.

- **Frankincense and Myrrh**

  Studies have repeatedly shown that smudging with frankincense and myrrh can kill harmful airborne bacteria. It is said that inhaled smoke can create white blood cells in your body, thus boosting your immunity to several diseases. Frankincense and myrrh also have anti-inflammatory properties and can even aid in getting rid of skin problems.

It goes without saying that no matter which herb, resin, or oil you use for smudging, some or the other of your physical ailments will most probably be healed. It may be a persistent skin rash, chronic sinusitis, recurring migraines, or even something as fatal as cancer.

Healing Spiritual Illnesses

Experts believe that physical diseases can trace their roots to your energy body. If harmful bacteria enter your system, their degrading effects are first apparent in your energy body before they affect your physical body. These effects are called spiritual illnesses, and they must be eliminated before you can be physically cured. That is exactly what smudging is most capable of doing.

The smudging process can detect the spiritual cause of your physical problems and wrench it out of your system before it causes your health to deteriorate any further. The negative energies present in your energy body are removed, leaving it ready and open to be filled with a burst of positive energy, healing all your spiritual illnesses. In short, smudging purifies your spirit, cleanses your energy, and heals your soul. It can cure illnesses by getting rid of the root cause. These causes include,

- **Ancestral Spirits**

  Did you recently make some of your ancestors unhappy? Did you do something that they would not have approved of? Then they might have cursed you with a physical disease you are currently suffering from. Smudging clears the negative energy from your ancestral spirits, bringing happiness back into their souls and curing you of the disease.

- **Household Spirits**

  Did you fail to follow the teachings of your household spirit? Your actions may have enraged that deity who, in turn, may have brought about some misfortune on your energy body. Smudging can eliminate that spiritual anger, cleansing and healing your energy body.

- **Harmful/Evil Spirits**

  There is a possibility that certain harmful spirits are circling you or your space, negatively affecting your spirit. Smudging can either remove the evilness from the spirits or eliminate them altogether. Either way, your spiritual health will be immensely improved.

- **Soul Loss**

  This is probably the worst spiritual illness you can experience. It implies what it states; the loss of your soul. Have you experienced some loss in real life? Maybe your loved one passed away, or you were the victim of an assault or an accident? Each real-life loss is believed to break the soul into fragments, eventually leading to complete soul loss (which leads to fatal, incurable diseases). Smudging heals your soul, mending each fragment and making it whole.

As you can see, your spiritual health directly affects your physical well-being. The purer your energy body, the better will your physical state be. And the process of smudging heals both bodies!

Healing Emotional Disorders

This is the most important and highly effective impact of smudging. As you might know by now, smudging focuses on removing the negative energy from a space or a person. And more often than not, that negative energy is created due to your negative emotions. Thus, it can be safely concluded that smudging heals emotional disorders from a space or a person. Indeed, emotional harmony is the smudging process's most conspicuous, immediately apparent result.

- **Anxiety**

  As healing emotional disorders is similar to all other types of physical healing, healing anxiety is similar to healing all other types of emotional disorders. As soon as you complete any of the smudging techniques, the first thing you will notice in yourself is the absolute lack of anxiety. It will be replaced by serenity so profound that all your other problems will seem to vanish into thin air (the problems may still be there, you just won't feel anxious about them).

- **Stress**

  On the surface, stress may seem no different from anxiety. After all, you feel anxious when stressed, and vice versa. But they are responses to entirely different situations. Anxiety is more of a fear of things that haven't yet happened, whereas stress is the pressure you feel about things you're currently experiencing. You can say that stress is a milder form of anxiety, but it can overwhelm and crush you if felt in excess.

  The soothing fumes surrounding you after smudging help reduce that stress, and the expunged negative energy wipes out the remaining pressure from your mind. You will start to think more clearly and manage your work and personal life more efficiently.

- **Depression**

This is one of the deadliest kinds of negative emotions. It can be fatal if left unchecked (leading to clinical depression). Unlike anxiety or stress, where you know outside factors are negatively affecting you, depression creeps up in complete secrecy, and, in this case, you are the one who is destroying your emotional state (no outside factors whatsoever).

When you are depressed, the negative energy almost always lies within you, not in the space around you or within other people. Smudging can help drive that energy out of you, expelling even those negative emotions that make you depressed.

- **Anger**

In a disturbed mind, anger is the most commonly felt emotion. Whenever you are nervous or stressed, you are often quick to feel anger. That is when the calming presence of smudging techniques shines best. The comforting smoke that wafts throughout the room enters your energy body and pushes out the anger-inducing negative emotions, creating a sense of peace within your soul. You may remember what you were angry about at the end of the process, but the situation won't allow you to feel that anger.

- **Hatred**

You may be feeling absolute, unrestrained hatred toward a person or a situation, so fiery and all-consuming that you may not feel love for anyone or anything else. Deep, intense hatred like this can be removed through smudging. At the end of the ritual, the state of oneness that you reach will help you forgive and forget the hatred for that person or place, replacing it with either apathy or love.

Other negative emotions, like guilt, frustration, jealousy, boredom, etc., can also be healed via smudging. Once the rituals are complete, you will reach an emotional balance with positive and negative emotions in equal measure, giving rise to a state of absolute calm. And if you look closely at the healing of emotions through smudging, you will realize that your emotional health depends on the strength of your spirit, which in turn depends on your physical well-being (and vice versa). It's all interconnected!

How to Heal with Smudging

The processes, techniques, and rituals of smudging remain the same, as detailed in the book's earlier sections. The only thing that changes is your *focus*. So far, you have been focusing on the general aspects of smudging, like believing that the negative energy in a space or within yourself is leaving. This time, you will need to focus on one form of negative energy during the smudging process.

Imagine that you wish to get rid of your anger. While beginning the smudging ritual and burning the herb, focus on pushing that anger out of your system. Concentrate on the chakras connected to anger (the one near the base of your spine and the other just above your navel) and believe they are being purified. That is how your anger will eventually subside into a sense of serenity.

In your astral/energy body, the chakras associated with emotions and diseases are,

1. **Root Chakra**

    Diseases: Arthritis, colon issues, constipation.

    Negative emotions: Anger, instability, fear, frustration.

2. **Sacral Chakra**

    Diseases: Lack of sexual drive, urinary tract problems, lower back issues.

    Negative emotions: Irritability, lethargy, manipulative tendencies.

3. **Solar Plexus Chakra**

    Diseases: Indigestion, diabetes, liver issues.

    Negative emotions: Low self-esteem, depression, rage.

4. **Heart Chakra**

    Diseases: Heart issues, weight instability, asthma.

    Negative emotions: Jealousy, dread, anxiety.

5. **Throat Chakra**

    Diseases: Thyroid problems, dental anomalies, breathing issues.

    Negative emotions: Inability to express your thoughts, introvert.

6. **Third Eye Chakra**

    Diseases: Headaches, migraines, hearing troubles, blindness.

    Negative emotions: Fear of success, selfishness.

7. **Crown Chakra**

    Diseases: Mental illnesses, nervous system imbalances.

    Negative emotions: Frustration, skepticism, suicidal tendencies.

You need to be at one with your energy body to be able to focus on your chakras. Each chakra should be clearly visible in your mind's eye; otherwise, this technique won't always work. That said, focusing on purifying your chakras is only one of the many healing methods with smudging.

- **Meditation**

Meditation literally means to focus on something for a set amount of time. You will need to clear your mind of all thoughts but one. For healing purposes, that thought should be part of your body, the type of spirit, or the kind of emotion you are trying to heal with smudging.

Another important part of meditation is your breathing. It should be slow and rhythmic. Breathe in, hold for a few seconds, breathe out, hold again, and repeat the process. A point to note: you must be experienced at smudging to heal using meditation techniques. That is because you don't want to be thinking about the ritual itself to make meditation successful. The acts of the ritual should be spontaneous, instinctual, and only one thought of healing should rule your state of mind.

- **Visualization**

This is almost the same as meditation. With visualization, you need to create a picture of the part of your body, spirit, or emotion you wish to heal. Thinking about it is one thing, but here, you need to believe that the part is actually in front of you. You can see it in your mind's eye, reach out for it and feel it. Let this feeling envelop your soul until you see nothing but the part to be healed. The smudging process will take care of the rest.

Consider that you wish to heal your diabetes. Begin the smudging ritual and visualize the diabetes in your body. Conjure up an image of the interior of your physical body. Imagine the blood flowing through your veins, as red as a beet in the sunshine. Now visualize the glucose as small yellow dots sprinkled throughout the bloodstream, like patches of weed on an otherwise fresh field. Finally, realize that the dots are diminishing, leaving your bloodstream.

Repeat this process during every one of your smudging rituals.

- **Prayer**

It is said that words are as powerful as visuals, and sometimes, they can move you more than an image ever could. And prayer can do wonders when you are using smudging to heal. It doesn't matter if it is a long, complex prayer suggested by a trusted shaman or a short, simple combination of words of your own making. What matters here is your understanding of that prayer and your belief in the words uttered. The stronger your belief, the more effective the ritual will be.

Assume that you wish to heal the suffering of your ancestral spirits. Let's say you have wronged them by taking your family business in a direction they don't like. In your prayer, start with an apology followed by an explanation, and end with a plea for forgiveness. It could go something like this,

> "O ancestral spirits (name them if you want), I'm sorry for my actions, but it was the best solution to find success in these trying times. Forgive me if you can."

Feel free to be more creative or even make poetry out of it. As long as you believe in the words and focus on bringing them to fruition, you can even sing them out loud! For healing, all that matters is your focus.

The Science Behind Healing with Smudging

You heard it right. Smudging is supported by science! The most fundamental science behind the ritual is that the smoke generated by smudging repels harmful bacteria from the environment. Studies have shown that more than 90% of bacteria is removed. Also, the smoke is easily absorbed into your system, reinvigorating your brain and bodily functions. Unlike tobacco smoke with a lethargic effect, the medicinal smoke of sage, cedar, or any other herbs makes you lively and energetic, ready to take on the world. The science behind that is the presence of negative ions in the smoke.

Don't worry! Negative ions aren't negative in the philosophical sense. When your body contains negative energy, it gets filled with positive ions (which are emotionally harmful). The negative ions released from the smudge smoke get absorbed into your body, canceling out the effect of the positive ions and opening up a door for positive energy to enter.

Smudging to Heal and Improve Holistic Health

Holistic health implies your overall health, including its physical, emotional, spiritual, intellectual, and social aspects. So far, you have learned how smudging can heal your physical, emotional, and spiritual being. Did you know that it can also rejuvenate the intellectual and social parts of your life?

When negative energy is removed from you and your space, your mind will be cleansed. This cleansing will allow you to analyze things objectively and heighten your faculty of reasoning. And that is exactly what a high level of intellect is! With this renewed clarity of knowledge, you can fill your cleansed mind with positive energy.

As you might have surmised, your social health depends on the kind of relationship you have developed with the people around you. Your social health is good if it is full of love and happiness. But your social health needs major improvements if it is rife with bickering and hostility. Smudging can heal your social life by removing the negative energy and emotions from your surroundings, yourself, and the surroundings and souls of your acquaintances, friends, and family.

In essence, smudging can heal your holistic health to improve your overall well-being. You can easily incorporate it into your daily wellness routine. Any time of the day or night is perfect for conducting the ritual. All that matters is your willingness to let go of the negative energy and your enthusiasm to invite positivity into your life.

Conclusion

Imagine this: After a long, exhausting day, you walk into your home, light up some sage, and let the fragrant smoke waft through the air. It's like a breath of fresh air, washing away all the stress and negative vibes that cling to you. Suddenly, your space feels lighter, calmer, and more inviting. It's as if smudging gives you a reset button, allowing you to leave behind the chaos and find a sense of peace within your surroundings. But smudging goes beyond creating a cozy atmosphere. It can also be a guiding light during times of change and transition. Smudging can be your faithful companion, whether moving to a new home, starting a new job, or going through a significant life change. It's like having a trusted friend who helps you let go of the past and embrace the possibilities of the future. With each swirl of the sacred smoke, you create a clean slate, inviting positive energy and new beginnings into your life.

And let's not forget about the spiritual side of smudging. It's like you have a direct line to your inner self and the greater universe. You're setting the stage for deep connection and self-discovery when you smudge before meditation, prayer, or any soul-searching practice. The gentle tendrils of smoke bridge the gap between the physical and the spiritual, helping you find a sense of harmony and unity within yourself. The best part? Smudging isn't just for spaces and rituals. It's adaptable to various situations. You can use it to cleanse and revitalize your cherished objects, such as your favorite crystals or sentimental jewelry, giving them a rejuvenating spa treatment, clearing away any lingering negative energy, and recharging them with positivity. And why not smudge yourself too? It will feel like you have a mini self-care routine for your energy field, allowing you to shed any heaviness and embrace renewed vitality.

So, as you close this book and end your exploration of smudging practices, remember this. It's not just a one-off practice; it's a way of life. It's about integrating smudging into your daily routine, like that cup of tea that brings you comfort and warmth each morning. By embracing the transformative power of smudging, you invite harmony, peace, and positive energy into your life. So go ahead, start smudging, and watch the magic unfold.

If you enjoyed this book, I'd greatly appreciate a review on Amazon because it helps me to create more books that people want. It would mean a lot to hear from you.

To leave a review:
1. Open your camera app.
2. Point your mobile device at the QR code.
3. The review page will appear in your web browser.

Thanks for your support!

Here's another book by Mari Silva that you might like

Your Free Gift
(only available for a limited time)

Thanks for getting this book! If you want to learn more about various spirituality topics, then join Mari Silva's community and get a free guided meditation MP3 for awakening your third eye. This guided meditation mp3 is designed to open and strengthen ones third eye so you can experience a higher state of consciousness. Simply visit the link below the image to get started.

https://spiritualityspot.com/meditation

Or, Scan the QR code!

References

"11 Popular Tarot Spreads for Beginners and Experts." Www.alittlesparkofjoy.com, 19 July 2021, www.alittlesparkofjoy.com/easy-tarot-spreads/#three-card-tarot-spread.

"13 Best Crystals for Divination." All Crystal, 9 Aug. 2022, www.allcrystal.com/articles/crystals-for-divination/.

"25 Types of Witches: The Magical List of Witchcraft." Facts.net, 4 July 2021, facts.net/types-of-witches/.

Aletheia. "7 Types of Spirit Guides (& How to Connect with Them)." LonerWolf, 5 Feb. 2018, https://lonerwolf.com/spirit-guides/

"Elemental Magic for Beginners: Basic Principles - Craft of Wicca." Craftofwicca.com, 8 Mar. 2019, https://craftofwicca.com/elemental-magic-for-beginners/#Elemental%20Magic%20For%20Beginners

"Gods and Goddesses in Witchcraft: A Beginner's Guide." Witchbox, 22 May 2023, https://witchbox.co.uk/blogs/witchbox-blog/understanding-the-13-gods-and-goddesses-in-witchcraft

Herbs, Colleen Vanderlinden Colleen Vanderlinden. "Evolution and History of Witchcraft Timeline." LoveToKnow, https://paranormal.lovetoknow.com/Witchcraft_History

"How to Cast a Wicca Ritual Magic Circle." The Not so Innocents Abroad, www.thenotsoinnocentsabroad.com/blog/how-to-cast-a-wicca-ritual-magic-circle.

https://www.facebook.com/learn.religions. "What's the Difference between Evoke & Invoke in Paganism?" Learn Religions, www.learnreligions.com/evoke-and-invoke-2561892.

"Learning Tarot: A Complete Tarot for Beginners Guide." Www.alittlesparkofjoy.com, 14 Sept. 2020, www.alittlesparkofjoy.com/tarot-beginners-guide/.

Leavy, Ashley. Crystal Divination: Three Techniques for Insight & Healing - Love & Light School of Crystal Therapy. 19 Aug. 2013, https://loveandlightschool.com/crystal-divination-three-techniques-for-insight-healing/

lynette_starfire. "List of the Most Used Gods in Witchcraft." Witches of the Craft®

"How to Do Ritual Magic - Gain the Power to Create the Life You Choose." Magic Self and Spirit, 14 Feb. 2020, www.magicselfandspirit.com/blogs/magic/how-to-do-ritual-magic/.

May 23, 2020 | Lifestyle. Types of Spirit Guides: The 11 Powerful Guides on Your Team - Typically Topical. https://typicallytopical.com/types-of-spirit-guides

"Moon Magic: A Beginner Crash Course in Lunar Witchcraft." Moody Moons, 4 July 2021, www.moodymoons.com/2021/07/04/moon-magic-a-beginner-crash-course-in-lunar-witchcraft/.

"Prehistoric Witchcraft - Magic Spells." Paranormal Knowledge, 25 Oct. 2020, www.paranormalknowledge.com/magic-spells/prehistoric-witchcraft.html.

"The Ultimate Guide to Magical Herbs for Spells & Rituals - TheMagickalCat.com." Www.themagickalcat.com, 18 Nov. 2020, www.themagickalcat.com/magical-herbs-guide.

"The Wheel of the Year Explained: The Ultimate Guide to Understanding Nature's Sacred Cycles - Small Ripples." Www.smallripples.com, www.smallripples.com/the-wheel-of-the-year-explained/.

Tyler, Deanna. "The Mystery of Nordic Rune Stones." Rune Divination, 18 Sept. 2015, https://runedivination.com/the-mystery-of-nordic-rune-stones/

"Wiccan Deities: A Complete Guide to Wiccan Gods and Goddesses." Explore Wicca, 8 July 2018, https://explorewicca.com/wiccan-deities/

WiseWitch. "Invoking the Gods & Goddesses: Common Sense Counsel." Wise Witches and Witchcraft, 3 Mar. 2018, https://witchcraftandwitches.com/gods-and-goddesses/invoking-gods-goddesses-common-sense-counsel/.

WITCH. "6 Elements (Yes, 6!) - How and Why to Invoke Them in Ritual." WITCH, 1 June 2016, https://badwitch.es/6-elements-yes-6-invoke-ritual

"Your Guide to Rune Divination." Rune Divination, 7 Oct. 2015, https://runedivination.com/your-guide-to-rune-divination

(N.d.). A-z-animals.com. https://a-z-animals.com/blog/jaguar-spirit-animal-symbolism-meaning/#:~:text=The%20jaguar%20is%20a%20symbol,intuition%2C%20confidence%2C%20and%20decisiveness

8 Reasons You Should Try Smudging & How To Do It At Home. (2017, May 8). Natural Living Ideas. https://www.naturallivingideas.com/smudging/

About sacred herbs & smudging ceremonies. (n.d.). Taosherb.com. https://www.taosherb.com/store/sacred-herbs.html

Acevedo, A. (2022, May 12). What is energy (as it relates to the law of attraction)? We explain. YouAlignedTM. https://youaligned.com/wellness/what-is-energy/

Amethyst - metaphysical healing properties. (n.d.). CRYSTALS & HOLISTIC HEALING. https://www.healingwithcrystals.net.au/amethyst.html

Amethyst meaning: Everything you NEED to know - healing properties & everyday uses. (n.d.). Tiny Rituals. https://tinyrituals.co/blogs/tiny-rituals/amethyst-meaning-healing-properties-and-everyday-uses

Askinosie, H. (2016, February 5). 8 ways to use crystals in your everyday routine. Mindbodygreen. https://www.mindbodygreen.com/articles/how-to-use-crystals-everyday

Ausler, N. (2022, December 4). 10 signs you're under A psychic attack & someone is sending you bad energy. YourTango. https://www.yourtango.com/self/signs-psychic-attack

Bauer, S. (2020, December 15). 10 of the incredible benefits of Palo Santo. Palo Santo Supply Company Ltd. https://palosantosupply.co/blogs/palo-santo/5-of-the-incredible-benefits-of-palo-santo

Beaulieu, C. (2022, August 13). 9 effective ways to protect yourself from psychic attacks. The Friendly Specter. https://www.friendlyspecter.com/9-effective-ways-to-protect-yourself-from-psychic-attacks/

Behind the meaning. (n.d.). Daisy London. https://www.daisyjewellery.com/blogs/our-world/behind-the-meaning-the-crown-chakra

Biancuzzo, M. (2022, April 5). 5 easy tips to help if you have trouble visualizing. Marie Biancuzzo, RN MS CCL IBCLC; MarieBiancuzzo.com. https://mariebiancuzzo.com/2022/04/05/5-easy-tips-to-help-if-you-have-trouble-visualizing/

Bihl, E. (2019, January 7). How to Smudge the Right Way (and Why You Should Do It). Brit + Co. https://www.brit.co/sage-smudging-tips/

Black Tourmaline Meaning: Healing properties & everyday uses. (n.d.). Tiny Rituals. https://tinyrituals.co/blogs/tiny-rituals/black-tourmaline-meaning-healing-properties-and-everyday-uses

Black Tourmaline. (2009). In Dictionary of Gems and Gemology (pp. 93-93). Springer Berlin Heidelberg.

Black Tourmaline: Meaning, healing properties, and powers. (n.d.). Mycrystals.com. https://www.mycrystals.com/meaning/black-tourmaline-meaning-healing-properties-and-powers

Bobb, B. (2022, August 10). Does burning sage really help you energetically cleanse your space? Vogue India. https://www.vogue.in/beauty/content/does-burning-sage-really-help-you-energetically-cleanse-your-space

Bolt, L. (2021, August 13). What is a spirit guide? Spirit guide meaning & more. Yahoo Life. https://www.yahoo.com/lifestyle/spirit-guide-spirit-guide-meaning-031900227.html

Bradford, D. (2023, January 1). How To Smudge Your House With Sage. Angels and Sages. https://angelsandsages.com/blogs/news/how-to-smudge-your-house-with-sage

Caron, A. (2021, September 23). Learn how to smudge. Seven Generations Education Institute. https://www.7generations.org/learn-how-to-smudge/

Chinnaiyan, K. (2017, February 23). 3 causes of self-doubt and how to conquer it for good. Tiny Buddha. https://tinybuddha.com/blog/3-causes-self-doubt-conquer-good/

Cho, A. (2012, July 7). Clear quartz meaning, healing properties, & uses. The Spruce. https://www.thespruce.com/what-is-a-clear-quartz-crystal-1274383

Cho, A. (n.d.). How to Smudge Your House to Invite Positive Energy. The Spruce. https://www.thespruce.com/how-to-smudge-your-house-1274692

Citrine - metaphysical healing properties. (n.d.). CRYSTALS & HOLISTIC HEALING. https://www.healingwithcrystals.net.au/citrine.html

Citrine meaning: Healing properties & everyday uses. (n.d.). Tiny Rituals. https://tinyrituals.co/blogs/tiny-rituals/citrine-meaning-healing-properties

Clear Quartz Meaning: Healing Properties & Uses. (n.d.). Tiny Rituals. https://tinyrituals.co/blogs/tiny-rituals/clear-quartz-meaning-healing-properties-uses

Coach, C. H. T. (1516444334000). Smudging - The science behind it. Linkedin.com. https://www.linkedin.com/pulse/smudging-science-behind-charmaine-howard

Dellner, A. (2018, April 26). What is energy work (and should I try it)? PureWow. https://www.purewow.com/wellness/energy-work

Detchon, A. (1528710839000). The importance of grounding and protecting your energy. Linkedin.com. https://www.linkedin.com/pulse/importance-grounding-protecting-your-energy-andrea-detchon-bsc-/

Dignity health. (n.d.). Dignity-Health.
https://www.dignityhealth.org/articles/what-is-holistic-health-care-anyway

Dimensions of wellness. (n.d.). Rwu.edu.
https://www.rwu.edu/undergraduate/student-life/health-and-counseling/health-education-program/dimensions-wellness

Energetic Harmony, let all your energy flow the right way. (n.d.). Attunements.
https://www.attunements.info/product/energetic-harmony/

Ferraro, K. (2022, December 31). 10 Easy Ways To Cleanse Your Home of Negative Energy. Mindbodygreen.
https://www.mindbodygreen.com/articles/how-to-cleanse-your-home-of-negative-energy

Five steps to deepen your relationship with your spirit guide. (n.d.). Kripalu.
https://kripalu.org/resources/five-steps-deepen-your-relationship-your-spirit-guide

Frankincense incense benefits: 12 crucial things to know. (n.d.). Tiny Rituals.
https://tinyrituals.co/blogs/tiny-rituals/frankincense-incense-benefits

Gemstone information - quartz Crystal Meaning and properties - fire mountain gems and beads. (n.d.). Firemountaingems.com.
https://www.firemountaingems.com/resources/encyclobeadia/gem-notes/gmstnprprtsrckc

Graham, M. (2020, May 21). Benefits of Smudging with Sage (5 Scientific Reasons to SMUDGE with Sage!). Tribal Trade.
https://tribaltradeco.com/blogs/smudging/benefits-of-smudging-with-sage-5-scientific-reasons-to-smudge-with-sage

Hannah, R. (1422379428000). What is A psychic attack? Linkedin.com.
https://www.linkedin.com/pulse/what-psychic-attack-raven-hannah/

How crystals can help you stay connected to your intentions. (2016, March 31). Mindbodygreen. https://www.mindbodygreen.com/articles/intention-setting-with-gemstones-crystals

How to Choose which Crystal is right for you ? (n.d.). Wands of Lust Co.
https://www.wandsoflust.com.au/blogs/news/how-to-choose-which-crystal-is-right-for-you

How to know if your crystals need charging + 9 potent methods. (2021, June 15). Mindbodygreen. https://www.mindbodygreen.com/articles/how-to-charge-crystals

How to make a DIY sage smudge stick. (n.d.). Rise Gardens.
https://risegardens.com/blogs/communitygarden/how-to-make-a-diy-sage-smudge-stick

Hurst, M. (2023, April 25). "Sound cleansing" - the easiest, most calming way to show negative energy the door. Homesandgardens.Com; Homes & Gardens. https://www.homesandgardens.com/life-design/sound-cleansing

Ibe, O. (2022, March 31). Earthing-A technique to help ground your body. Verywell Mind. https://www.verywellmind.com/what-is-earthing-5220089

Jain, R. (2020, October 8). Crown Chakra: Discover the divine energy of Sahasrara chakra. Arhanta Yoga Ashrams. https://www.arhantayoga.org/blog/crown-chakra-divine-energy-of-sahasrara-chakra/

Jay, S. (2022, August 3). 6 Cleansing Rituals For You & Your Home. Revoloon. https://revoloon.com/shanijay/cleansing-ritual

Jones, L. (2023, January 28). 35 grounding techniques for upsetting thoughts. Claritytherapynyc.com. https://www.claritytherapynyc.com/35-grounding-techniques-for-upsetting-thoughts/

Joseph, B. (2017, February 16). A Definition of Smudging. Ictinc.Ca. https://www.ictinc.ca/blog/a-definition-of-smudging

Julie. (2022a, February 5). Black Tourmaline meaning. Moonrise Crystals. https://moonrisecrystals.com/black-tourmaline-meaning/

Julie. (2022b, February 5). Selenite meaning. Moonrise Crystals. https://moonrisecrystals.com/selenite-meaning/

Julie. (2022c, February 6). Rose Quartz meaning. Moonrise Crystals. https://moonrisecrystals.com/rose-quartz-meaning/

Kyla. (2022, July 19). Aura Cleansing Spray - DIY Sage Spray for Spiritual Cleansing + Protection. A Life Adjacent. https://alifeadjacent.com/aura-cleansing-spray/

Lagman, R. (2021, July 13). Smudge prayer examples - part II: What to say when you're smudging to get rid of spiritual energy. Tribal Trade. https://tribaltradeco.com/blogs/teachings/smudge-prayer-examples-part-ii-what-to-say-when-you-re-smudging-to-get-rid-of-spiritual-energy

Lashi, B. (n.d.). Life Organic Blog [Organic Beauty/Minimalism/Wellness]. Embodyzen.Com. https://www.embodyzen.com/blog/8-step-smoke-bathing-ritual

Lim, E. (2021, November 6). How to create a personal energy shield for protection via visualisation. ILLUMINATION. https://medium.com/illumination/how-to-create-a-personal-energy-shield-for-protection-via-visualisation-23c8af69be56

Loewe, E. (2021, June 24). 5 Spiritual Smudge Sprays That Are Sustainable Or Indigenous-Made. Mindbodygreen. https://www.mindbodygreen.com/articles/smudge-sprays-what-they-are-4-to-start-with

M., X. (2020, April 2). Smudging for Healing. Villagerockshop.com. https://www.villagerockshop.com/blog/smudging-for-healing/

Maclean, L. (2021, March 22). 7 signs you're under psychic attack & how to stop it (2023). Mysticmag.com; MysticMag. https://www.mysticmag.com/psychic-reading/3-signs-youre-under-psychic-attack/

Majsiak, B., Young, C., & Laube, J. (n.d.). A beginner's guide to breath work practices. Everydayhealth.com. https://www.everydayhealth.com/alternative-health/living-with/ways-practice-breath-focused-meditation/

Marci. (n.d.). Smudge Prayer to Invoke the Four Directions. Marci Cagen. https://marcicagen.com/smudge-prayer-to-invoke-the-four-directions/

McKnight, J. (2020, December 5). 3 effective empath shielding meditations. Planet Meditate. https://planetmeditate.com/empath-shielding-meditation/

McQuerry, L. (n.d.). Make your own Smudge Stick. Moon Magic Co. https://moonmagic.co/blogs/news/make-your-own-smudge-stick

Morning, J. (2021, November 15). What is grounding, and how can it help me? Spunout. https://spunout.ie/mental-health/self-care/what-is-grounding

Natural essential oil pure blend smudging sage - island essentials: Natural body & hair care products. (2021, July 12). Island Essentials: Natural Body & Hair Care Products - Natural Body & Hair Care; Island Essentials. https://islandessentials.ca/shop/island-essentials/essential-oils-carrier-oils/essential-oils/essential-oil-blends/natural-essential-oil-pure-blend-smudging-sage/

Nesci, N. (2020, March 4). 5 things everyone needs to know about energy healing. The Growth & Wellness Therapy Centre. https://www.growthwellnesstherapy.com/our-blog/5-things-everyone-needs-to-know-about-energy-healing

No title. (n.d.). Pranaworld.net. https://pranaworld.net/what-is-the-energy-body/

O'Connor, B. (2015, November 23). 7 sacred resins to burn for clearing negative.... Spirituality+Health. https://www.spiritualityhealth.com/blogs/your-creative-spirit/2015/11/23/bess-oconnor-7-sacred-resins-burn-clearing-negative-energy

Obsidian - metaphysical healing properties. (n.d.). CRYSTALS & HOLISTIC HEALING. https://www.healingwithcrystals.net.au/obsidian.html

Obsidian meaning. (n.d.). Anahana.com. https://www.anahana.com/en/lifestyle/crystals/obsidian-meaning

Obsidian meaning: Healing properties & everyday uses. (n.d.). Tiny Rituals. https://tinyrituals.co/blogs/tiny-rituals/obsidian-meaning-healing-properties-everyday-uses

Ohren, K. (2021a, August 8). Citrine healing properties, meanings, and uses. Crystal Vaults. https://www.crystalvaults.com/crystal-encyclopedia/citrine/

Ohren, K. (2021b, August 11). Black Tourmaline healing properties, meanings, and uses. Crystal Vaults. https://www.crystalvaults.com/crystal-encyclopedia/black-tourmaline/

Page, K., & Jane, P. (2017, December 9). 30 sacred herbs for smudging and cleansing purposes. Ilmylunajane. https://www.ilmylunajane.com/single-post/2017/12/09/30-sacred-herbs-for-smudging-and-cleansing-purposes

Pollard, S. (2020, October 13). Make your own smudge sticks to banish bad energy. Hello Nest. https://hellonest.co/diy-smudge-sticks/

Pollard, S. (2022, January 12). How to make your own Rosemary sage Smudge Sticks. Hello Glow. https://helloglow.co/how-to-make-your-own-rosemary-sage-smudge-sticks/

Proctor, B. (2022, April 11). The law of attraction vs. The law of vibration. Proctor Gallagher Institute. https://www.proctorgallagherinstitute.com/47878/the-law-of-attraction-vs-the-law-of-vibration

Regan, S. (2022, April 26). How To Make Your Bath A Spiritual Experience: 16 Tips & Techniques. Mindbodygreen. https://www.mindbodygreen.com/articles/spiritual-bath

Regan, S. (2023, May 10). How Sound Baths Are Revolutionizing Healing + How To Try One For Yourself. Mindbodygreen. https://www.mindbodygreen.com/articles/sound-bath

Rekstis, E. (2022, November 15). Healing Crystals 101: Everything you need to know.

Ress, J. (2019, March 29). How To Use the Healing Powers of Quartz Crystals. SpaGoddess Apothecary. https://spagoddess.com/blogs/spagoddess-wellness-blog/clear-quartz-crystals

Richards, D. (2000). Rose Quartz. Daphne Richards.

Robby. (2021, February 27). The Benefits of Smudging: Why It's an Ancient Tradition. Dr. Lam Coaching – World Renowned Authority on Adrenal Fatigue Recovery. https://www.drlamcoaching.com/blog/benefits-of-smudging/

Rooted Revival. (2023, April 10). 9 sensational cedar smudge stick benefits. Rooted Revival. https://rootedrevival.com/cedar-smudge-stick-benefits/

Rooted Revival. (2023, June 9). 12 fantastic lavender smudge stick benefits. Rooted Revival. https://rootedrevival.com/lavender-smudge-stick-benefits/

Rose Quartz Meaning: Healing properties and everyday uses. (n.d.). Tiny Rituals. https://tinyrituals.co/blogs/tiny-rituals/rose-quartz-meaning-healing-properties-and-everyday-uses

Rose quartz: Meaning, healing properties and powers. (n.d.). Mycrystals.com. https://www.mycrystals.com/meaning/rose-quartz-meaning-and-healing-properties

Ryan, K. (2019, April 29). Supercharge: What you need to know about cleansing crystals. Wanderlust. https://wanderlust.com/journal/supercharge-what-you-need-to-know-about-cleansing-crystals/

Sake, F. P. (2017, September 12). Thirteen Quick Ways to Cleanse Energy. For Puck's Sake. https://www.patheos.com/blogs/matauryn/2017/09/12/thirteen-quick-energy-cleanse/

Salt Water Bath: A Cleansing, Healing, And Nourishing Ritual For Your Mind And Body. (n.d.). Linkedin.Com. https://www.linkedin.com/pulse/salt-water-bath-cleansing-healing-nourishing-ritual-your-mind-/

Salzberg, S. (2022, November 14). How to meditate. Mindful; Mindful Communications & Such PBC. https://www.mindful.org/how-to-meditate/

Selenite meaning: Healing Properties & everyday uses. (n.d.). Tiny Rituals. https://tinyrituals.co/blogs/tiny-rituals/selenite-meaning-healing-properties-everyday-uses

Short, E. (2021, November 10). 7 signs of negative energy in a person. Mål Paper. https://malpaper.com/blogs/news/7-signs-of-negative-energy-in-a-person

Signs of negative energy. (n.d.). WebMD. https://www.webmd.com/balance/signs-negative-energy

Son, N. T. (2023, March 14). 20 how many crystals are there? Advanced Guide 07/2023. Soccercentralph. https://thcsnguyenthanhson.edu.vn/20-how-many-crystals-are-there-advanced-guide/

Spiritual illnesses. (n.d.). Stanford.edu. https://geriatrics.stanford.edu/ethnomed/hmong/fund/spiritual_illnesses.html

Stelter, G. (2016, October 4). Chakras: A beginner's guide to the 7 chakras. Healthline. https://www.healthline.com/health/fitness-exercise/7-chakras

StMU. (2021, September 27). Sweet Grass. StMU; St. Mary's University. https://stmu.ca/sweet-grass/

The College of Psychic Studies : Enlighten : What is a psychic attack. (n.d.). The College of Psychic Studies. https://www.collegeofpsychicstudies.co.uk/enlighten/what-is-a-psychic-attack/

The complete guide to smudging. (n.d.). JL Local. https://jllocal.com/blogs/articles/2

The Sacred Art of Smudging. (n.d.). Kripalu. https://kripalu.org/resources/sacred-art-smudging

Theodora Blanchfield, A. (2022, January 31). How to meditate with crystals. Verywell Mind. https://www.verywellmind.com/how-to-meditate-with-crystals-5214020

TIMESOFINDIA.COM. (2020, September 12). How to identify negative energies at your home and remove them. Times Of India. https://timesofindia.indiatimes.com/life-style/home-garden/how-to-identify-negative-energies-at-your-home-and-remove-them/articleshow/78075353.cms

UPLIFT. (2017, August 8). The science behind smudging. UPLIFT. https://uplift.love/the-science-behind-smudging/

Ward, K. (2021, December 14). How to program a crystal with your intention, because yes, you should be doing that. Yahoo Sports. https://sports.yahoo.com/program-crystal-intention-because-yes-173400639.html

What Is Shamanic Smudging? (n.d.). Incensewarehouse.Com. https://www.incensewarehouse.com/What-Is-Shamanic-Smudging_ep_30-1.html

White, A. (2018, July 18). 10 benefits of burning sage, how to get started, and more. Healthline. https://www.healthline.com/health/benefits-of-burning-sage

Williams, R. (2018, July 17). Enhance your meditation practice with crystals. Chopra. https://chopra.com/articles/enhance-your-meditation-practice-with-crystals

Willis, K. K. (2016, January 18). Grief and rage: The connection between 4th and 1st chakras. Lucid Body | Acting Classes and Coaching for the Physical Actor. https://lucidbody.com/blog/grief-and-rage-the-connection-between-4th-and-1st-chakras/

Image Sources

[1] *Metropolitan Museum of Art, CC0, via Wikimedia Commons:*
https://commons.wikimedia.org/wiki/File:%22Diana,_Goddess_of_the_Hunt%22,_Folio_from_the_Davis_Album_MET_DP107569.jpg

[2] https://commons.wikimedia.org/wiki/File:Wheel_of_the_Year.svg

[3] *Jakub Jankiewicz (Jcubic), CC0, via Wikimedia Commons:*
https://commons.wikimedia.org/wiki/File:Five_elements_and_pentagram.svg

[4] https://commons.wikimedia.org/wiki/File:Triple-Goddess-Waxing-Full-Waning-Symbol.svg

[5] https://commons.wikimedia.org/wiki/File:Venus_and_Adonis.jpg

[6] https://commons.wikimedia.org/wiki/File:Gavin_Hamilton_-_Apollo_and_Artemis,_1770.jpg

[7] https://commons.wikimedia.org/wiki/File:Theodoor_van_Thulden_-_Athena_and_Pegasus_(1654).jpg

[8] *Gunawan Kartapranata, CC BY-SA 3.0 <https://creativecommons.org/licenses/by-sa/3.0>, via Wikimedia Commons:* https://commons.wikimedia.org/wiki/File:Bastet.svg

[9] https://commons.wikimedia.org/wiki/File:Marduk_and_pet.jpg

[10] https://commons.wikimedia.org/wiki/File:Thecomingofbrideduncan1917.jpg

[11] https://commons.wikimedia.org/wiki/File:Ceridwen.jpg

[12] https://commons.wikimedia.org/wiki/File:Tanz_der_Dryaden.jpg

[13] https://commons.wikimedia.org/wiki/File:Dakshina_Kali_-_19th-century.jpg

[14] https://commons.wikimedia.org/wiki/File:Die_Nornen_Urd,_Werdanda,_Skuld,_unter_der_Welteiche_Yggdrasil_by_Ludwig_Burger.jpg

[15] https://unsplash.com/photos/fzMgicYhJws

[16] https://www.pexels.com/photo/runic-letters-on-wood-chunks-and-ground-with-autumn-leaves-10110445/

[17] https://commons.wikimedia.org/wiki/File:Black_Rune_5.svg

[18] Ekirahardian, OFL <http://scripts.sil.org/cms/scripts/page.php?item_id=OFL_web>, via Wikimedia Commons: https://commons.wikimedia.org/wiki/File:RUNIC_LETTER_URUZ_UR_U.svg

[19] https://commons.wikimedia.org/wiki/File:Runic_letter_thurisaz.png

[20] File:B_rune_short-twig.png: User:Skadinaujovectorization:Own work, Public domain, via Wikimedia Commons: https://commons.wikimedia.org/wiki/File:B_rune_short-twig.svg

[21] Original uploader Berig, GFDL <http://www.gnu.org/copyleft/fdl.html>, via Wikimedia Commons: https://commons.wikimedia.org/wiki/File:R-runes.png

[22] Ekirahardian, OFL <http://scripts.sil.org/cms/scripts/page.php?item_id=OFL_web>, via Wikimedia Commons: https://commons.wikimedia.org/wiki/File:RUNIC_LETTER_K.svg

[23] Ekirahardian, OFL <http://scripts.sil.org/cms/scripts/page.php?item_id=OFL_web>, via Wikimedia Commons: https://commons.wikimedia.org/wiki/File:RUNIC_LETTER_HAEGL_H.svg

[24] https://commons.wikimedia.org/wiki/File:Runic_letter_naudiz.png

[25] Ekirahardian, OFL <http://scripts.sil.org/cms/scripts/page.php?item_id=OFL_web>, via Wikimedia Commons: https://commons.wikimedia.org/wiki/File:RUNIC_LETTER_ISAZ_IS_ISS_I.svg

[26] https://commons.wikimedia.org/wiki/File:Runic_letter_ar.svg

[27] Haisollokopas, CC BY-SA 4.0 <https://creativecommons.org/licenses/by-sa/4.0>, via Wikimedia Commons: https://commons.wikimedia.org/wiki/File:Sowilo_(alternate).svg

[28] https://commons.wikimedia.org/wiki/File:Tiwaz_rune.svg

[29] Ekirahardian, OFL <http://scripts.sil.org/cms/scripts/page.php?item_id=OFL_web>, via Wikimedia Commons: https://commons.wikimedia.org/wiki/File:RUNIC_LETTER_BERKANAN_BEORC_BJARKAN_B.svg

[30] Ekirahardian, OFL <http://scripts.sil.org/cms/scripts/page.php?item_id=OFL_web>, via Wikimedia Commons: https://commons.wikimedia.org/wiki/File:RUNIC_LETTER_MANNAZ_MAN_M.svg

[31] Ekirahardian, OFL <http://scripts.sil.org/cms/scripts/page.php?item_id=OFL_web>, via Wikimedia Commons: https://commons.wikimedia.org/wiki/File:RUNIC_LETTER_LAUKAZ_LAGU_LOGR_L.svg

[32] Ekirahardian, OFL <http://scripts.sil.org/cms/scripts/page.php?item_id=OFL_web>, via Wikimedia Commons: https://commons.wikimedia.org/wiki/File:RUNIC_LETTER_RAIDO_RAD_REID_R.svg

[33] https://unsplash.com/photos/g95sf8-fEQg

[34] Rob Lavinsky, iRocks.com – CC-BY-SA-3.0, CC BY-SA 3.0 <https://creativecommons.org/licenses/by-sa/3.0>, via Wikimedia Commons: https://commons.wikimedia.org/wiki/File:Apophyllite-54502.jpg

[35] Ivar Leidus, CC BY-SA 4.0 <https://creativecommons.org/licenses/by-sa/4.0>, via Wikimedia

Commons: https://commons.wikimedia.org/wiki/File:Azurite_-_New_Nevada_Lode,_La_Sal,_Utah,_USA.jpg

[36] Rob Lavinsky, iRocks.com – CC-BY-SA-3.0, CC BY-SA 3.0 <https://creativecommons.org/licenses/by-sa/3.0>, via Wikimedia Commons: https://commons.wikimedia.org/wiki/File:Calcite-20188.jpg

[37] Didier Descouens, CC BY-SA 4.0 <https://creativecommons.org/licenses/by-sa/4.0>, via Wikimedia Commons: https://commons.wikimedia.org/wiki/File:Herkimer.jpg

[38] Linas Juozėnas, CC BY-SA 4.0 <https://creativecommons.org/licenses/by-sa/4.0>, via Wikimedia Commons: https://commons.wikimedia.org/wiki/File:Picture-jasper.jpg

[39] Adam Ognisty, CC BY-SA 3.0 <https://creativecommons.org/licenses/by-sa/3.0>, via Wikimedia Commons: https://commons.wikimedia.org/wiki/File:2_lapis_lazuli.jpg

[40] Eric Polk, CC BY-SA 4.0 <https://creativecommons.org/licenses/by-sa/4.0>, via Wikimedia Commons: https://commons.wikimedia.org/wiki/File:Opal_NHMLA.png

[41] https://commons.wikimedia.org/wiki/File:Turquoise.pebble.700pix.jpg

[42] https://unsplash.com/photos/83SUHaReev4

[43] https://unsplash.com/photos/SzwyWBHwLMk

[44] https://unsplash.com/photos/0-c1F9uukx8

[45] https://www.pexels.com/photo/man-falling-carton-boxes-with-negative-words-7203956/

[46] https://unsplash.com/photos/WzrOg4YzJ5w

[47] https://unsplash.com/photos/r3_ZiorB_Ik

[48] https://unsplash.com/photos/zVsQmJEd_DA

[49] https://unsplash.com/photos/Tinbs_bjKxA

[50] https://unsplash.com/photos/78EiTnCtn5U

[51] https://unsplash.com/photos/96zlc1Bt51w

[52] https://unsplash.com/photos/x5hyhMBjR3M

[53] https://unsplash.com/photos/Hn4wYHOaeIc

[54] https://unsplash.com/photos/pIY5yM0bmMQ

[55] https://unsplash.com/photos/k65_6C4hu2E

[56] Marie-Lan Taÿ Pamart, CC BY 4.0 <https://creativecommons.org/licenses/by/4.0>, via Wikimedia Commons https://commons.wikimedia.org/wiki/File:Amethyst_Siberia_MNHN_Min%C3%A9ralogie.jpg

[57] Jan Helebrant, CC BY-SA 2.0 <https://creativecommons.org/licenses/by-sa/2.0>, via Wikimedia Commons https://commons.wikimedia.org/wiki/File:Schorl_black_tourmaline_-_NaFe2%2B3Al6(BO3)3Si6O18(OH)4_(28838960018).jpg

[58] https://unsplash.com/photos/vxf-uurQ5rY

[59] Bergminer, CC BY-SA 4.0 <https://creativecommons.org/licenses/by-sa/4.0>, via Wikimedia Commons https://commons.wikimedia.org/wiki/File:Rose_quartz_Spain.jpg

⁶⁰ *Rama, CC BY-SA 3.0 FR* <https://creativecommons.org/licenses/by-sa/3.0/fr/deed.en>, *via Wikimedia Commons* https://commons.wikimedia.org/wiki/File:Citrine_quartz-AMGL_79477-P5030194-black.jpg

⁶¹ *B. Domangue, CC BY-SA 4.0* <https://creativecommons.org/licenses/by-sa/4.0>, *via Wikimedia Commons* https://commons.wikimedia.org/wiki/File:Obsidian_-_Igneous_Rock.jpg

www.ingramcontent.com/pod-product-compliance
Lightning Source LLC
Chambersburg PA
CBHW051854160426
43209CB00006B/1300